Managing in virtual organizations

Managing in virtual organizations

Malcolm Warner and Morgen Witzel

THOMSON

Australia • Canada • Mexico • Singapore • Spain • United Kingdom • United States

Managing in virtual organizations

Copyright © Thomson Learning 2004

The Thomson logo is a registered trademark used herein under licence.

For more information, contact Thomson Learning, High Holborn House, 50–51 Bedford Row, London, WC1R 4LR or visit us on the World Wide Web at: http://www.thomsonlearning.co.uk

British Library Cataloguing-in-Publication Data
A catalogue record for this book is available from the British Library

ISBN 1-86152-984-8

Typeset by Dexter Haven Associates Ltd, London

Printed by Seng Lee Press Pte Ltd, Singapore

Contents

The impact of virtuality on organizing: what restructuring is needed and what will it cost? 127
The impact of virtuality on staffing: how will people work and be rewarded? 128
The impact of virtuality on directing: where does the 'buck' stop? 129
The impact of virtuality on co-ordinating: who paints 'the big picture'? 130
The impact of virtuality on reporting: who reports to whom, and where does the information go? 130
The impact of virtuality on budgeting and finance: how are assets valued? 131
Conclusion 132

11 The virtual general manager 134

Defining the virtual general manager 134
Virtual management gaps 136
New tasks for virtual management 137
Training and education for virtual general management 139
Teams in virtual general management 142
Creating a virtual management culture 143
Conclusion 144

12 Summing up 147

The virtual mix 148
Who should go virtual? 149
What are the implications of going virtual? 150
Conclusion 151

Bibliography 153
Index 159

Preface

T he virtual organization as a business concept is still very much in its infancy. It has been theorized about, albeit to a limited extent, and in the mid-to-late 1990s a number of papers, articles and books were produced which talked up the idea of virtual organization and forecast it to be the organizational way of the future. Many of these books were wildly over-optimistic, especially in terms of the length of time it would take for the virtual organization to become widely accepted. Then came the bursting of the dotcom bubble, and with it an equal and opposite overreaction set in; the virtual organization was just another high-tech fantasy, and would never catch on.

This book is an effort to set the record straight. The virtual organization is feasible and does offer many benefits, especially if the idea is viewed pragmatically and implemented in a way that complements the existing organization, adding value rather than destroying it. The virtual dimension offers huge potential for growth, but managers have to be careful not to 'throw the baby out with the bath water'. Nor is virtual organization cost-free. There can be huge costs associated with moving into the virtual dimension, of which technology costs are usually just the tip of the iceberg.

Most of all, however, if virtual organizations are to succeed, those responsible for their management have to get used to the idea of managing in a new way. In making the transition to virtual organization, psychology is more important than technology. Managers need to understand what the virtual dimension is, and what its crucial components may be, including intangible capital. They need to understand what goes on in virtual space, including the critical role played by knowledge flows and knowledge transformation. Only when they have thoroughly explored the boundaries of this new realm can they go about setting up systems and organizations. Would a manager move into a new market in East Asia or South America without first gathering as much information as possible, not only about the market and competitors but also about culture, management and organization in those new environments? The answer is no – and the same is true of the virtual dimension.

This book was written partly to encourage managers to look at virtual organization as a strategic option, and partly to show how management in virtual organizations relates to management in conventional organizations. Readers may be surprised to find that there is both continuity and discontinuity; some aspects of managing in virtual organizations look wholly different, others look startlingly familiar.

At times this book may seem overly cautious. But a degree of caution is surely warranted; the events of the last three years show what happens when managers plunge ahead without due regard for principles, for planning, for measured analysis and thinking. But despite this, we believe the virtual organization offers real possibilities, for individual firms and for whole economies. We urge this book to be read, not as a road map to competitive success, but as a summing up of critical issues and a call for action upon them.

This book has been some years in the making, and we are grateful to the publishers of some our previous efforts in the *Journal of General Management*, *Human Systems Management* and *Corporate Finance Review* for allowing us to re-use some material here. Thanks too must go to the *International Encyclopedia of Business and Management* team, notably the former in-house project editor, Tara Montgomery, and the current one, So-Shan Au. The *IEBM* not only brought the authors together as a working team for the first time, but the experience of developing it – of working in a genuine virtual environment – sparked off many of the first ideas that later germinated in this book. At Thomson Learning, too, we would like to thank Anna Faherty who first commissioned the book, and all those who have worked with us on the project since, particularly Geraldine Lyons and Giulia Vincenzi.

Malcolm Warner
Morgen Witzel
December 2002

Figures and tables

1 Introduction

Virtual organization is the newest and potentially most important form of business organization to have emerged for decades. Enabled by, and driven by, new information and communications technologies, most importantly the Internet, the virtual organization model offers businesses a chance to reduce costs, become more flexible and extend their market reach all at once. Assets may be dispersed rather than concentrated; the importance of physical location in determining effectiveness has been greatly reduced. The swift interchange of information allows people to work together in teams even if they are thousands of miles apart. Customers can be reached and goods and services sold to them without the selling firm ever seeing the customer or physically handling the goods. The opportunities are enormous. The 'new' technology appears to be creating a 'new' economic form. The benefits have been lauded and 'hyped'; in the late 1990s in particular, much investment was elicited and expectations ran high. Everything about these novel organizations was described in hyperboles. It was all larger than life.

And yet, the risks too are very high. Virtual organizations are, by their very nature, largely intangible, and human beings – especially those raised and educated in the West – are not very good at managing those things that they cannot see, hear and feel. Managing in virtual organizations is a complex task. It is not that managing a virtual business is entirely different from managing a conventional firm: indeed, all the same old tasks such as marketing, financial management and accounting, operations management and human resource management (HRM) are still required. But the nature of these tasks changes in virtual organization, and further sets of tasks – most importantly, knowledge management – are also required. It is hard to say which is more dangerous: failure to master the new techniques required for management in virtual organizations, or failure to understand that the old skills remain vitally important for business success.

Management in virtual organizations is management-plus. It requires adherence to business fundamentals and a grasp of the new environment, an ability not only to use technology but also to 'think virtually', to work in a world where imagination and creativity are essential but where hard data and facts have lost none of their cogency. There is a balance that must be struck, and failure to get the balance right often means business failure as well.

The bursting of the dotcom bubble in 2000 and 2001 brought many of these issues into sharp relief. For a time, even, the financial press and others turned against the idea of the virtual organization. 'Bricks, not clicks' became a mantra for those who doubted the potential of e-commerce and other firms of virtual organization ever to deliver. But as is now recognized – thanks in part to revealing biographies of these firms and their founders such as *Burn Rate* and *Boo Hoo* (Wolff 1999; Portanger 2002) – most of these firms failed not because they were dotcoms, but because they were badly managed from the outset. They were also badly financed. By this, we do not mean that they were underfinanced; often, quite the contrary. But the players in the dotcom market, including bankers and venture capitalists, operated under the delusion that they were in an entirely new world and that the old rules of business did not apply. They financed ventures that under other circumstances, they would never have touched.

But not every dotcom business failed. The well-managed ones, particularly those in the business-to-business (B2B) market, stuck it out and even prospered (see *The Economist*, 18 November 2000). And another phenomenon emerged: the traditional firm that also diversified into e-commerce and showed that it is possible to make money doing both at once. Barnes and Noble, the New York bookseller which also sells online, may have a lower market capitalization than Amazon.com; but it also makes more profit. Suddenly a new model, of 'bricks and clicks', began to be talked about. Was this really a new world, was it the same old world with new rules, or was it, in fact, a new world but one where the old rules, or some of them at least, still applied? Had economics as previously defined in effect been proved obsolete?

The consideration of virtual organization vs 'real' organization is not a case of black vs white. What we see instead are differing shades of grey. Virtual organizations have many of the same traits as their conventional counterparts: they require finance, they are staffed by people, they sell products and services to customers. To repeat: all the old skills of management are still required, and businesses neglect these at their peril. Yet virtual organizations are different places, and other skills such as communication, learning and the assessment and valuation of knowledge shift from the periphery of management to occupy a central place. Virtual organizations offer huge potential, but to make them work and to realize their value, virtual managers will have to be even more highly skilled, even more professional and even more hard working than their conventional counterparts.

There is a distinction we can make between investment in new technology ('lumps' of resources invested at any given time) and the persistence of the 'use-value' of the innovation after the event. There were, to use an analogy, booms and busts during the early days of the railways, but the actual physical plant of the railways, and the managerial and organizational innovations that accompanied them, remained after the low point of the cycle and provided the infrastructure for the next stage of economic expansion. The same could be said of the later advances in communications, such as the telegraph, telephone and so on. We must always distinguish between the short-term cycle and the longer-term 'wave'. Thus, though the first 'wave' of virtual organizations ended in large-scale disappointment, the technologies and techniques developed then remain with us, and remain of value.

Virtual organization is not a formula for painless success; adopting the concept will not automatically bring lower costs and higher profits. Rather, virtual organization is a complex idea that needs to be implemented with great care, and like all complex concepts, it is not risk free. The aim of this book is to explain the fundamental nature of the virtual organization, to highlight some of the risks and pitfalls and show how these can be avoided, and to show how successful management in virtual organizations requires the learning of new skills, while ensuring at the same time that the old ones are not neglected.

Defining the virtual organization

As noted above, the concept of the virtual organization has been around for a decade or more, and there is already a sizeable literature on it. For example, Barnatt (1995) and Bleeker (1998) have looked at the technological bases for the growth of virtual organizations and described how they are enabled by communications technology, in particular. Writers on organization, including Grenier and Metes (1995), Goldman *et al.* (1995) and Dunbar (2001), have looked at what virtual organizations do, how they are structured and how they function. The late Edith Penrose (2001) briefly discussed the virtual organization as one of the new types of firm emerging from networking, and this has been taken up by later writers such as Franke (1999, 2002) concerning concepts such as the virtual web organization. Meanwhile, Osborne (2001) and Pennings (2001) have discussed the virtual firm as the logical conclusion of present trends in strategy and innovation. Franke (2002:i), reviewing the latest developments in the field, thought there would be 'benefits for all parties concerned'.

Definitions of the virtual organization are understandably often 'fuzzy'. This is not surprising, as the concept itself is a deliberately formless and fluid one which aims, in part at least, to get away from the rigid hierarchies and bureaucracies that often characterize conventional organizations. Rather than trying to come up with a single definition of what a virtual organization is, we are probably better off noting the features that nearly all virtual organizations have in common:

- Lack of physical structure: virtual organizations have a lower physical presence than their conventional counterparts. They have fewer tangible assets such as office buildings, warehouses etc., and those they do have are often geographically dispersed. In operating terms, small, decentralized offices are favoured over large, concentrated ones. Bleeker (1998:44) describes virtual firms as 'defined not by concrete walls or physical space, but by collaborative networks'. Barnatt (1995), taking the trend to its logical extreme, goes so far as to suggest that in the future firms may be structured entirely in virtual reality formats; computer links will take the place of physical infrastructure and firms will exist only in cyberspace. Economies of scale here are almost inevitable.

- Reliance on communications technologies: Goldman *et al.* (1995:205) define the virtual organization as 'a new organizational model that uses technology to dynamically link people, assets and ideas'. But they add that, 'although technology will be an important facilitating mechanism for the virtual organization, in the long run, it will not be an essential requirement.' Modern information and communications technology play a vital role, and are seen by many as being at the heart of the whole concept of the virtual organization. And on one level, this is quite true. The Internet, and other technologies now being developed and launched, appear to be of critical importance. Every organization needs a framework, to define it and give it shape. Conventional organizations use physical structures, such as office buildings; virtual organizations use networks of communication for the same purpose. Yet, when all is said and done, technology is a tool, an enabler. It facilitates the organization, but it is not the organization itself, any more than an office building can be said to 'be' or 'represent' a conventional organization.

- Mobile work: the use of communications networks rather than buildings and physical assets means that the physical location of work is now less important. As a result, departments and teams no longer have to work in close contact with each other. Project teams can be – and in industries such as publishing, routinely are – assembled from persons in different countries or on different continents, who work together but never come into physical contact. Nor need work be carried out within the confines of the traditional office. Bleeker (1998) comments that, increasingly, the office is where the worker is and not vice versa. Costs can be reduced dramatically as a consequence. Office space in Central London cost about £10,000 (or about US$16,500) per employee in 2002, but provision of home-working equipment could cut this by more than a third.

- Hybrid forms: Grenier and Metes (1995) refer to virtual organizations as hybrids, and Goldman *et al.* (1995:202) refer to virtual organizations primarily as collaborative agencies, the integration of 'core competencies, resources and customer market opportunities'. Franke (1999, 2002) defines what he calls the 'virtual web organization', consortia of companies and business units working together within a loose framework to achieve a mutual goal. Such hybrids can be short term, such as limited-life consortia brought together to undertake costly and risky research and development (R&D) projects, or they can be longer term in orientation, such as virtual supply chains (Schary and Skjøtt-Larsen 2001). Again, costs per employee and project can fall substantially as a result.

- Boundaryless and inclusive: related to the above is the fact that virtual organizations are deliberately fuzzy in nature. They are not limited to what we think of as individual companies or corporations as defined by law (and herein, of course, lies another level of complexity). They can, and often do, encompass suppliers and distributors, with links in the supply chain so tight that it can be difficult to see where one firm ends and another begins. They can also encompass customers: drawing on the services marketing concept that the customer is part of the production process (Bateson 1995), they build organizations in which customer and provider are tightly linked and the participation of each is required to make the service work. Online financial services are perhaps the most developed example of this phenomenon. Unit costs again may accordingly fall, and it is thus that many banking institutions are offering, for example, better interest rates for online accounts.

- Flexible and responsive: virtual organizations can – in theory at least – be quickly pulled together from a variety of disparate elements, used to achieve a certain business goal and then dismantled again. They can also be quickly restructured and assets redeployed to meet changing strategic needs. Because transaction costs are lower, there are fewer costs and fewer risks involved in making a radical change of direction. Of all the claims made for the virtual organization, however, it is this one that may be the most contentious. The potential for flexibility is obviously there, but to achieve it requires a countervailing flexibility on the part of the organization's managers and its employees. New kinds of HRM strategies are needed to deal with these innovations. Employees have to be selected who can work more flexibly, for example.

Purpose and structure of virtual organizations

Just like their conventional counterparts, virtual organizations have two key characteristics: they have a purpose and they have a structure.

Four decades have passed since the well-known Harvard business historian Alfred Chandler commented that for firms to achieve success, structure must follow strategy (Chandler 1962). Although the statement has since been qualified by business-school critics such as Henry Mintzberg (1989), the basic principle continues to hold good. In order to find the 'right' structure, an organization must first know what its goals are and what it must achieve. It then tries to find the optimum structure for efficient achievement of those goals. We humbly follow this logic in this monograph.

It may seem trite to say as much, but this alignment is every bit as important for virtual organizations as it is for conventional ones. Virtual organization is not a goal in itself: converting to a virtual form does not mean the 'end of management' or the fulfilling of the business's ultimate aims. In strategic terms, virtual organization needs to be seen as a strategic option. Moreover, it is an option that should be taken if and when managers have analysed the needs of the business and its customers and determined that the virtual option would fulfil those needs better than a conventional organizational form would.

Moreover, as we shall argue repeatedly throughout this book, for managers, 'Should we go virtual?' is not a one-time-only question. The analysis needs to be applied not just to the firm as a whole, but to individual business units, processes, departments and functions. Very few firms are actually suited to complete 'virtuality' – that is, virtual organization applied to every aspect of their business: finance, supply, production, marketing etc. Some physical presence, some geographical concentration point, will always be needed. General Motors, which has a very advanced virtual supply-chain network, nevertheless must concentrate final production and assembly at fixed points: cars cannot be built in virtual space. The same applies to publishing houses, which commission and, increasingly, distribute books using virtual networks, but still require printing and warehousing facilities to handle the final product. The fact that many publishers are also developing e-books and e-magazines merely reinforces the point made above: no major publisher is making a success of e-publication on its own, and a twin-track strategy is vitally necessary. On another dimension, retail banks, which now manage the bulk of their back-office functions virtually, still find it necessary to maintain conventional 'shop windows' for many of their customers.

It thus follows that managers need to develop organizations which have both virtual and tangible components, the exact mix of which will depend on the needs of customers and suppliers, the nature of the product or service the company produces and the value it adds. These components should fit together into an organizational form that is fit for the purpose and able to achieve its goals. The decision as to 'virtual or tangible' applies to two dimensions: the organization's assets, and the organization's management structure. Table 1.1 below shows how these dimensions fit together.

In the table, cell 1 represents cases where organizational assets are virtual in nature and are managed in a virtual way. Examples could include dispersed sales teams that are managed remotely by telephone and Internet. Many financial services firms also fall into this category, with dispersed networks of offices around the globe trading a largely virtual commodity – financial instruments – over the wire.

Cell 2 represents tangible assets that are nonetheless capable of being managed in a virtual fashion. Perfect examples of this form of organization are rare, and most feature robotic or remotely controlled technology; a famous example is the Mars Rover programme, in which a remotely piloted vehicle gathering data on one planet was controlled from a base on another planet. However, global virtual supply chains, such as are common in the car and computer industries, conform to some extent to this type. Micro-processors and other semiconductors may pass through as many as four or five different production facilities – often in as many different countries – as they move down the value chain through the various processes of etching, masking and so on to finished status. The physical production plants are controlled 'virtually' from the corporation or supply-chain headquarters.

Cell 3 represents cases where virtual assets are managed in a tangible way. A simple example is manual work on computer databases; data has to be input by

Table 1.1 Organizational assets and management structure

Management	Virtual	Tangible
Virtual	1	2
Tangible	3	4

a human operator sitting at a desk with a keyboard or other user interface, but the data being input is stored virtually in the computer's electronic memory. Old-style publishing houses and other companies in the business of creating and selling intellectual property often fit into this cell; they make and sell intangibles, but do so using concentrated physical facilities. Finally, corporate training centres and other educational institutions frequently operate in this way with learning concentrated at a single site, though increasingly these are tending to use virtual management and delivery systems (cell 1).

Cell 4 represents cases where tangible assets are manipulated and managed in a tangible way. This is the conventional organization as we know it, physically and hierarchically concentrated. Examples include old-style production-line work by companies such as steelmakers or shipbuilders.

This model shows how different asset forms and different management processes can impact on each other and be combined into different organizational forms. Yet the choice of real vs virtual is not even as simple as trying to pick the right cell in the diagram above. Most complex organizations – and most large organizations are complex – will fit into more than one of the cells, depending on the business function being examined. As the case of the publishing project at the end of this chapter shows, the mix of tangible and virtual assets can change as a project goes forward, or as market needs change and new opportunities open up. It is perfectly possible for the same company, at the same time, to be managing a virtual R&D project as part of a consortium (cell 1), to be operating a virtual supply chain and distribution system (cell 2), to be undertaking training programmes for staff at a corporate learning centre (cell 3) and to be producing products on an old-fashioned assembly line (cell 4).

To repeat, the choice of 'real', 'tangible' or 'conventional' vs 'virtual' is not one that can be made uniformly for an entire company and all of its operations. Every organization has both virtual elements (the knowledge capital possessed by the organization and inherent in its people, machines and records) and tangible elements (the physical factors of production, the machinery and technology it uses to maintain its networks and people). The strategic and organizational solution to an organization's needs lies in getting the mix right. There are few, if any, bespoke solutions. Every organization is unique, and every organization needs to find the right mix that will meet its goals and – importantly – be suited to the capabilities of its managers.

When we speak of virtual organization, we are speaking of 'organization with virtual elements' (or, if preferred, of 'virtual organization with tangible elements'). The distinction may seem unimportant, but it is not. The continuing presence of the tangible world in virtual organizations means that, as well as learning the new skills they require when dealing with this new environment, managers also need to continue to learn and practise the basic skills of management. Virtual organization represents evolution, not revolution: a progressive development of organizational form, not a complete break from what has gone on before. Nowhere is this more evident than when we consider the uses virtual organizations make of technology.

Hard and soft technology in the virtual organization

As noted above, virtual organizations are to a large extent enabled by information and communications technology. Today, that technology consists of Internet and, increasingly, broadband communications technology. It is worth noting, however, that successful virtual organizations have been established using other technologies. A couple of historical examples may clarify. Reuters news agency was established in the 1850s to provide an intangible product (news information) through a dispersed network (the telegraph system) and fits quite closely with the definition of cell 1 above. In 1940, the Royal Air Force (RAF) fought a successful battle against the numerically superior Luftwaffe using a virtual control network enabled by two technologies – radio and radar – which co-ordinated tangible resources – men and fighter planes – at decisive points, not dissimilar to cell 2 above. So, there is not necessarily a computer-driven model behind what we can conceptualize as a virtual system.

Nevertheless, the advent of the Internet made virtual organization much easier and more practical for many businesses. Information could be retrieved, exchanged and analysed more quickly, and in far greater quantities. This had several immediate consequences. In economic terms, the new technology allowed companies to reduce internal transaction costs, both directly, through costs savings (e-mail is cheaper than an internal postal system, even though many companies continue to maintain both), and indirectly, by speeding up information transactions and saving time. In organizational terms, it increased the managerial span of control in terms of physical space, allowing managers to contact and stay in touch more easily with colleagues and subordinates in physically distant places. The telegraph and the telephone had already done this to some extent, but Internet and intranet systems had a number of features, such as the ability to handle multiple users easily, that had been lacking before.

This in turn has led to a reversal of a century-long trend towards concentration and hierarchy aimed at creating economies of scale. In the early twentieth century, firms sought to grow and create economies of scale in part in order to 'internalize' – to use Alfred Chandler's term – functions which had formerly been undertaken out of house, so as to reduce transaction costs and increase competitiveness. But, paradoxically, reducing transaction costs also often meant reducing flexibility and efficiency as large organizations became stiff and bureaucratic. The new technology offered a chance for businesses to have their cake and eat it too. Peripheral business activities could be sent out of house once more, allowing organizations to scale down and concentrate on their core business while at the same time kept transaction costs low (or at least, lower than the corresponding added value the organization was able to provide).

All this, plus an understandable human tendency to become overexcited about the potential of new ideas, has led to the identification by many of virtual organizations with their hard technology: that is, their computers, software, cabling and other devices that maintain their communications networks. As noted above, Barnatt (1995) even argues that it is possible to have a 'complete' virtual organization that is free of all human activity and which exists entirely in cyberspace, while Michael Dell (1999) has also mused on the prospects of management becoming entirely a 'virtual' function.

This idea might work well in science fiction, but is unlikely to see much implementation in practice. To be sure, there are some systems, such as feedback and control mechanisms, which exist entirely in a virtual world, and experiments with artificial intelligence, if successful, could mean that human input in some areas is lessened still further. But in general, technology systems cannot and do not function on their own. Technology is an artefact. On its own it is inert and of no value. An empty office is a charge upon an organization's accounts regardless of how much technology is stuffed into it until people come to use it. Technology requires agency, and in the world in which we live at present, that agency can only come from human beings.

Thus, on the one level, technology has greatly increased and enhanced our ability to do business virtually, and has created an apparent revolution in how and where we work. But at the same time, it has done so not by overturning all of the old certainties about management – some, to be sure, but not all – but by providing us with a powerful tool which we can use to manage more effectively. Management has always been mostly about people, and it still is. It is for this reason that Goldman *et al.* (1995) argue that while technology is important to virtual organizations, it is not essential.

It is human beings, 'soft' technology, whose brains and sense and hands continue to manage, direct and staff business organizations, and it is human beings who continue to be their customers. It seems unlikely that it will ever be possible to entirely eliminate them from either role. So long as this remains the case, therefore, managers in virtual organizations will need to strive to find a second balance, in addition to the one noted above: between the needs and/or utility of people and those of machine technology.

For human beings too work in virtual space. Machines create virtual space – or have it created for them – by networks of communication. People also create virtual space, using their own memories and imaginations. All of us store, retrieve and use virtual data, information and knowledge in our working lives, and we do so not only as individuals but also as groups and teams. Max Boisot (1995) has referred to what he calls 'information space', a kind of realm of the imagination which exists in every organization and is a core part of its culture, determining what kinds of knowledge and information are transmitted, how and to whom. As we will argue in detail later in this book, Boisot's theory is important: IT, which greatly amplifies the speed and scale of information interchange, also magnifies the effects of information space. In highly bureaucratic organizations, for example, IT can be used as kind of controlling or gatekeeping mechanism and can actually serve to reduce some information flows. Not all virtual spaces are happy places to be. Depending on how they are constructed and the purposes they are intended to serve, they can be free, creative and exciting places to work, or they can be what Gareth Morgan (1986) so eloquently describes as 'psychic prisons', where imagination and flexibility are restricted and inhibited. It only remains to quote one further literary authority, Jean-Paul Sartre: 'Hell is other people'.

The dystopia Sartre was describing was one which is created in the mind, not through any physical punishments.

The greatest challenge facing managers in virtual organization is the management of the interface between 'soft technology', people, and other physical systems. People and technology function according to fundamentally different rules; computers and software, as electronic-mechanical systems, can be replicated and will function in the same way, while people, as biological organisms, are each unique. There is a tendency to fall back on the reliability of electronic-mechanical technology and to create systems to which the human element will hopefully be forced to conform (automatic telephone systems which offer callers 'options' depending on what services they might or might not want are a crude example of this). We will argue later that such systems fall into many of the same traps as the proponents of scientific management did a century ago, attempting to reduce human behaviour to mechanical rules. The best systems, as the cyberneticist Alexander Kolmogorov (1965) pointed out, are also the most complex ones, as they allow for the maximum number of possibilities for human–machine interface and can therefore process a maximal amount of information and knowledge.

Knowledge and value

The idea of the virtual organization overlaps with several other recent management concepts, notably knowledge management and the learning organization. The idea of the latter goes at least as far back as North American management gurus, Peters and Waterman (1982), who used the phrase 'learning organization' to denote companies that invested in research and development and viewed knowledge as an organizational asset. (The phrase 'thinking organization', current in the 1920s, expressed some of the same ideas.) The notion that knowledge could be considered an asset in its own right came to the fore with the work in the late 1980s of Arie de Geus and Peter M. Senge at Royal Dutch/Shell and MIT, and it was de Geus (1988) who made the now famous statement that in the future a company's only sustainable competitive advantage may be its ability to learn faster than its competitors. This in turn led to the idea of 'knowledge capital', knowledge as a factor input on the same basis as the traditional factors of production, land, labour and (money) capital. Knowledge capital was seen by Davis and Meyer (1998), for example, as being related to other concepts such as human capital and organizational capital, a relationship which is described in more detail below. Warner and Witzel (1998) suggested that one of the key tasks of the general manager was the acquisition, use, creation and diffusion of knowledge within the firm, and went on (1999) to develop a model of knowledge production and dissemination. On a broader scale, Albert and Bradley (1997) have commented on the rise of knowledge-based industries, showing how knowledge is being used to create and add value in a variety of economic settings.

The relationship of these developments to virtual organizations is simple: the technology networks on which these organizations are founded exist to transmit knowledge. This knowledge can take a variety of forms, ranging from hard data such as financial or market statistics, to received knowledge disseminated in a variety of forms. According to Japanese management scholars Nonaka and Takeuchi (1995), networks can be used not just to circulate but to directly create knowledge. In either case, however, as founder of the computer company that bears his name, Michael Dell, (1999) astutely pointed out, it is the function of networks to transmit knowledge.

Knowledge is the lifeblood of the virtual organization. To call it 'knowledge capital' seems almost to undersell its importance. Knowledge is not only a factor input; its creation, transmission and use is implicit in almost everything a virtual organization does. Turning off the flow of knowledge would be akin to turning off the mains power and physically switching off the network. If there is no knowledge to transmit, then the network is idle and useless; the managers and employees who work at its various nodes are effectively isolated and powerless. A graphic example of this occurred in Manhattan on 11 September 2001, when terrorist attacks destroyed the World Trade Centre and forced the evacuation of many other office buildings in New York's financial district. In all but the buildings directly affected by the attack, the communications infrastructure remained in place. But with no people on site to use it, the network was virtually dormant and activity in the financial community ground to a halt for several days.

How does this differ from conventional organizations? These latter, too, rely on knowledge: on the skills of their employees, on managers' knowledge of the market, on researchers' ability to innovate new products and improve existing ones, and so on. The differences are not so much in the importance of knowledge itself, which was recognized as long ago as the nineteenth century by economists such as Nassau Senior and Karl Marx, but rather in the kinds of knowledge that are wanted and the ways in which knowledge is used. And, just as technology networks are inert without knowledge to pass along them, so in virtual organizations knowledge is all but useless unless the networks exist along which it can be transmitted. In conventional organizations there are a variety of ways in which to transmit knowledge, including face-to-face conversations and meetings. In virtual organizations, where people are working in remote locations or buying from remote sites, everything depends on the network's ability to handle knowledge and transmit it in an intelligible form. The role of technology, then, is crucial not only as an enabler but also because, if wrongly handled, it can shut doors and cut off knowledge flows, leaving employees and customers out of the loop and in the dark.

Technology and knowledge are two important ingredients in the virtual organization recipe. Neither, however, will become active without the addition of the third important element, people. It is no accident that new theories such as the learning organization and knowledge capital/knowledge management put such a strong emphasis on the human element of organization. The same must be true of the virtual organization. We argue that virtual organization, far from stating the primacy of technology, is in fact primarily a human-centred concept in which the management of people is more important than the managing of technology, but in which neither can be wholly separated from the other.

Managing in virtual organizations is not about either one, but both; it is the management of people managing technology.

The structure of the book

These, then, are the major themes on which this book depends. We begin with the building blocks of virtual organization by looking in more detail at the role played by technology in creating virtual organizations and the concept of 'virtual space' in which they exist. Chapter 2 defines virtual space, while chapter 3 explains the role played by 'hard technologies' such as computer systems in creating and defining it. Chapter 4 then brings in the role of 'soft technologies' – people – the relationship they have with hard technology, imagining the implications of this for management.

Having defined the parameters of virtual organizations, we then go on to look at the role played by knowledge in making them function. The interrelated roles played by knowledge capital, human capital and organization capital are discussed in chapter 5, while chapter 6 looks at the sources of these kinds of capital and their relationship to other factors of production such as land, labour and finance. Chapter 7 then describes the knowledge transformation process, the mechanism whereby knowledge is turned into value, and shows how virtual organizations function through a constant transformation of knowledge which passes through and along their networks.

The next four chapters focus specifically on the challenges of management in virtual organizations. Chapter 8 begins by describing a conventional model of general management, the POSDCORB model derived from the work of the French management thinker, Henri Fayol (1917), and show how this applies in conventional firms. As will be apparent from the discussion, management in these firms has a high level of knowledge requirement and has many 'virtual' features. Referring to the discussion above, we note that physical assets can be managed in a virtual way, and indeed vice versa. How managers conceptualize their conventional role will have implications for how they go on to manage in virtual space.

Chapter 9 considers in more detail the notion of virtual organization as a strategic option. It suggests the development of a value-creation matrix in which physical/virtual options can be considered across the range of the company's products/services and markets. That choice can be made along any or all of six dimensions: value, control, efficiency, innovation, motivation and relationship-building, each of which is discussed in detail.

Chapter 10 then looks at the problems of managing within virtual organizations, and applies the management model given above. Virtual operations will have an effect on all the key tasks of management: planning, organizing, staffing, directing, co-ordination, reporting, and budgeting and finance. We consider the problems that are posed for each. Chapter 11 then assesses the differences between management in virtual and conventional organizations and suggests that managers used to working in the latter will need to bridge a series of 'gaps' in order to be effective in the former. These include the need for new skills, the ability to design and implement networks, the ability to manage knowledge effectively, the ability to manage outside the firm (whose boundaries may become increasingly fuzzy) and the ability to manage and control from the centre-outwards rather than the top-down. We go on to suggest that the conventional tasks of management described above need to be supplemented by a further set of tasks and related skills, summarized in the acronym CALV (communications, assessment, learning, valuation).

We conclude by showing how managers, especially general managers, are the pivot on which the whole virtual organization depends. The implication is that in order to be effective in virtual organizations, managers will have to become even more professional and highly skilled than before. They will need a strong balance of technical and human, hard and soft skills, and will need to be able to think holistically as well as functionally. They will need to be able to find the right balance between control and creativity, and to be able to design organizations that are both strong and flexible, that serve customers and support employees. The virtual organization offers a new approach to management that could open the door to competitive success and lasting profitability. But this approach is a complex one, and only those managers able to find the kind of balances we describe here will be able to succeed.

Case Study *International Encyclopedia of Business and Management*

From the early 1990s to 1996, the authors of this book were involved in the publication of the first edition of the *International Encyclopedia of Business and Management*, a major publishing project in the field of business reference.[1] Malcolm Warner was earlier on the scene as the editor-in-chief, while Morgen Witzel joined a little later (working with the in-house editor, Tara Montgomery) as a member of the editorial/production team established by the publisher. The finished product consisted of six volumes with 5523 pages. Around 470 authors contributed over 500 articles. A second and expanded edition in eight volumes was published in 2002, containing over 750 entries.

The management and execution of the project had a number of virtual features, but the nature of these features and the relationship between virtual

[1] The *IEBM* could theoretically have been produced without modern information technology. Previous reference books of this type such as the *Dictionary of Industrial Administration* (1928), edited by John Lee, were produced using only telephone and surface mail networks. This was a much smaller project than the *IEBM*, however, and took longer to produce. Technology speeded up the production process and also rendered it more technically efficient, giving greater scope to the complementary skills of the authors, editors and production team.

and tangible assets and management changed over the course of time. The project began with the appointment of Professor Warner as editor-in-chief and the subsequent appointment of an editorial advisory board and then of 13 subject editors responsible for individual fields or disciplines. This editorial board contacted and recruited authors, who were then provided with guidelines and contracts from the project administrative office at Routledge. At this stage, the project was very much in cell 1 (virtual management of virtual assets). The authors were located at universities and professional institutions in Europe, Asia, Australia and North and South America. Few had ever met Professor Warner or been to the publisher's office in London, and there was virtually no face-to-face communication with any of the parties: e-mail, supplemented by telephone, fax and surface mail, provided most of the project infrastructure. While some previous projects may have been carried out without much direct contact, this was a 'first' for Routledge in terms of the scale of the endeavour.

The second phase began when authors had submitted their finished articles and editorial and production work began. This phase fits into cell 3 (physical management of virtual assets). An in-house production team based at Routledge and numbering around 20 people edited the articles and typeset them. Unusually for that time (1995–6), all the editorial and production work was done on screen, with hard copies of articles being generated only at the end of this process.

The third phase fits into cell 2, the virtual management of physical assets. Before going to press, every article was printed out in its final form and sent to the editor-in-chief for inspection and for the adding of additional material such as cross-references. Copies of individual entries were also sent to their authors by post or fax, and copies were also sent to out-of-house freelance proofreaders for checking. This progress of the paper artefacts, totalling nearly 17,000 pages, was tracked and monitored as they were printed out, sent to authors and proofreaders and returned with any final corrections; authors and proofreaders who were late in replying were reminded by telephone or e-mail.

The fourth phase fits into cell 4, the physical management of physical assets. This phase consisted of the production of the final finished artefacts, the books themselves. After all final corrections were taken in and the volumes were sent for printing and binding, emerging in 1996 as the finished six-volume set ready to be delivered to customers. These stages were completed almost exactly on time and on budget.

The final phase saw a return to cell 1, as the publishers began developing plans for an electronic version of the encyclopedia, and plans were also put in motion for the development of supplementary volumes. Soon after, development of the second edition, ultimately published in hard copy in 2001, was commenced, starting the cycle over again.

Thus over the course of a few years, the nature of the project assets changed several times: from intangible, largely uncodified knowledge in the minds of the project team members, to codified and tangible knowledge embodied in artefacts (the printed proofs and finally the printed and bound volumes). As the nature of the assets changed, so too did the management approach, which at times used a virtual network model and at times concentrated resources in a single physical location according to the needs of the project.

Source: M. Warner (2001), 'Introduction' to *International Encyclopedia of Business and Management*, 2nd edn, London: Thomson Learning, pp. ix–xiv.

Making virtual space

2 Creating and managing virtual space

Virtual organizations exist partly within virtual space. They are, as we pointed out in chapter 1, a relatively 'new' phenomenon, but they also have their roots in earlier developments. In technical terms they use mental and technological constructs to represent certain aspects of organization that, in more conventional organizations, have a physical existence (and most organizations, to be realistic, still take this form). In other words, in virtual organizations the solid physical realities of bricks and mortar, offices and production plants, colleagues and customers met face to face, are, to some extent – sometimes to a large extent – dissolved and replaced by virtual forms. Solid blocks become fine networks. Instead of managing within organizations that enclose us and envelope us, we are part of an organization that is fluid, flexible and to a large part invisible, and which can be called into existence only by active mental effort on our part. In virtual space, we place less emphasis on our five physical senses, and much more on our inner knowledge and imagination. It is an organizational 'brave new world' of sorts, one that many still find it difficult to come to terms with.

The purpose of this chapter is to look at virtual space and to describe it in managerial terms. We begin by discussing the nature of human space, and go on to describe virtual space as resting on three other 'spaces', one defined by technology, the other two by human and cultural factors. We show not only how virtual space is developed, but also how a variety of technological and human factors can serve to limit its bounds. Finally, we conclude the chapter by looking at some of the main managerial issues and constraints which make managing virtual space as hard as – if not harder than – management in more conventional conditions. In particular, management in virtual space requires a constant series of trade-offs between the freedom and flexibility that virtual space offers and the basic, age-old managerial needs for accountability, planning and structure.

It is sometimes argued that virtual space is created by communications technology. That is not strictly speaking true. Technology, as we will see in chapter 3, enables virtual space, but it does not create it *per se*. People create virtual space: they imagine it, then build or install the technology to maintain it. It is unlikely that without the advances in IT over the last two decades or so that virtual space could have diffused as extensively as it has. Yet database software does not create databases on its own; human operators do that, using the database software as a tool. And in order to do so, they must first work out how the database will be structured: how many fields there will be, what those fields will be, and so on.

In order to create a virtual organization, therefore, it is first necessary to create the virtual space in which that organization exists. Only then can the relevant technology be designed and applied. Virtual space requires not only IT but also human imagination. It is 'radically new' and not 'merely novel', to use the terms employed by Graham (1999) in his short but insightful work, 'The Internet'. It is transformative and even revolutionary. It is 'power to the people' (1999:38). It challenges the 'physical space' demarcations of the nation-state and is the true precursor of globalization. Most of important of all, perhaps, it offers a new opportunity for businesses and managers to overcome some of the constraints of their present markets and environments, if they can make the successful transition to managing in virtual space.

This chapter describes virtual space, how it is created and some of the problems of managing in a virtual way. Later chapters take up these problems one by one and look at some potential solutions. For the moment, though, let us concentrate on describing what virtual space is and how it is created.

Conventional space vs virtual space

Every organization requires 'space'. Organizational life is anchored not only in time through which its functioning unfolds, but also in space. This dimension can take many forms, and often takes several of these forms simultaneously. There is, for example, the physical space defined by walls and boundaries within which business is conducted: these include office buildings, factories, warehouses and the like. On top of these, however, exist layers of other 'spaces', which are created by the ways in which the members of the organization define it, think about it and act within it. Boisot (1995) describes these conceptualizations as the 'information space' of an organization, and links it intrinsically to the organization's culture. Gareth Morgan, in his *Images of Organization* (1986), writes of multiple metaphors of organization that are linked to the ways in which individuals see organizations and react to them. Metaphors help us come to grips with organizational reality.

Virtual space partakes of both these concepts. It is in part a substitute for (or replica of) physical space, substituting technology such as communications systems for bricks and mortar. At the same time, it is very much an imagined or mentally created space, which requires a mental effort to summon up. Workers on an assembly line do not have to 'imagine' their work; it comes to them, and they are merely required to carry out a set of routine tasks that have been laid down for them by a higher authority. Workers in a virtual organization, if they are to carry out their tasks at all, have to 'imagine' the organization around them, and must be able to think about the network and know which parts of it to use in order to carry out their tasks. Grasping the organizational reality around one focuses action to achieve specific goals.

To show how this works in practice, take a common example of a virtual firm, the Internet retailer. The managers in an Internet retailer never see their customers; they have no idea what they look like. They have some information about those customers, but often not much; e-mail addresses don't provide the same basis for analysis as postal codes, for example, so geographical analysis is not available unless the retailer remembers to ask customers for their addresses and/or postal codes. Buying patterns offer some clues, but these take time to form into patterns. The Internet retailer does not have the advantage of daily, face-to-face customer contact that the manager of a corner shop or a restaurant has.

As a result, the Internet managers' need to imagine their customers is much greater. Of course there is a difference here between 'imagine' and 'imaginary': Internet managers do not have imaginary customers (though reading some of the accounts of the dotcom collapses in the previous chapter might convince the reader otherwise). Customers are real, but without any direct contact, the Internet retail manager has to use his or her imagination to create an image of the absent customer and his or her wants and needs. For this reason, many Internet retailers try to get around this problem by creating virtual customer communities or other similar devices for maintaining contact with customers and getting feedback. But these virtual communities also require an effort of imagination to sustain them. Unless all involved, company and customers, feel themselves part of the community and are willing to participate actively in it, it will wither and die.

Organizations that exist in physical space are characterized by large physical facilities. Often these are centrally located, keeping communications paths to a minimum. They have large offices or plants in which numbers of staff work in close physical proximity. They tend also to have large, pyramidal hierarchies as described in the classical writings on bureaucracy of German sociologist, Max Weber (see Weber 1947) writing at the beginning of last century. This is the way in which most large corporations were structured – many still are – and the advantages of this form are well known. They include efficiency, economies of scale thanks to internalized operations and easier co-ordination and control. Directions, once given, are carried out promptly. And, although such organizations can often become machine bureaucracies, many employees and managers feel more secure in such organizations, although insecurity is becoming more of a feature of everyday life in Western industrial societies than it was. They implied, in their day – often wrongly – a sense of permanence. Employees knew where they were, to whom they reported and who reported to them. But their weaknesses included not only the bureaucratic nature noted above, but high overhead costs and a heavy reliance on functionalization and division, which can stifle flexibility and creativity (for examples of this argument see Peters and Waterman 1982; Kanter 1983; Pennings 2001). Their 'space' is real and tangible and requires no great effort to imagine and understand; it can also be taken for granted.

Organizations that exist in virtual space are, by contrast, characterized by having few physical facilities, and those that do exist are often widely dispersed. They are typically creatures of their age and characterize the late twentieth century and its innovatory values. They are often 'young' organizations and are found in 'turbulent' environments where broader environmental and techno-logical changes are impacting on companies and their markets. Their strengths are the increased flexibility and creativity that comes from the network style of organization. Management tends to be centre-outward rather than top-down. There is less of a premium on data, and more of a premium on knowledge, which encourages creativity. Lack of internal – or even external – boundaries means the organization can be reconfigured quickly, while the externalizing of many functions offers the chance to concentrate on the business core. But, the lack of physical structure and geographical dispersal also create problems. Motivation is one such problem; the flexibility of virtual organizations is perceived by many as instability, and this can create barriers. Risk-averse investors may feel that they are not investing in anything tangible; risk-averse employees may feel that they have less security. While many people may be happy to become transient workers or managers, hopping from one job to another as the opportunities arise, others find this style of working worrying and threatening (Handy 1996). What Bridges (1995) has called the 'death of the job' is a fearful prospect to many.

There are also problems of control and accountability, as it is more difficult to supervise people who are working remotely. As we shall discuss below, these problems can be solved to some extent by the application of technological systems for control, but there is a danger here; too much control can rob the virtual organization of the very flexibility it was set up to create, by hindering employee initiative and telling people what they can and cannot do. There is also a tendency to try to create virtual systems that are 'simple' and easy for employees to buy into. This again may be going in the wrong direction. As the cyberneticist Alexander Kolmogorov (1965) has pointed out, the 'best' virtual systems – that is the ones capable of processing the most knowledge and therefore the most flexible – are also the most complex. Kolmogorov notes that degrees of complexity and degrees of flexibility are closely linked, just as an animal with more vertebrae in its spinal column can bend more easily than one with fewer.

The 'space' in which virtual organizations exist, then, is not visible to the naked eye. It cannot be seen, touched or felt; only the artefacts that create it, such as computers and people, can be visualized. The connections between them, between the nodes of the network, can be spelled out in diagrams and models, but these are only static representations: it still requires knowledge and imagination to understand these and make them function. But as Graham points out (1999:151–52), 'what is imaginable is not necessarily conceivable'. Virtual space, then, has its limits; imagination is essential but cannot take us easily to the next steps. 'Organizational imagination' is not normally a concept found in organization behaviour textbooks.

Therefore, the creation of a virtual organization does not mean just setting up a computer network and then building an organization around it. It requires first of all an act of creativity, the creation of the virtual space in which the organization will function. This requires 'special' people with 'special' skills. We are embarking into a new dimension of human capital here.

Generating virtual space

Although, as noted, organizations have many spaces, there are three particular types of space that are used to create virtual space. These are:

- imaginary space, which is defined by the organization's levels of inherent knowledge and creativity;
- technology space, which is defined by the organization's technological capabilities (including systems capacity but also human operator skills);
- cultural space, what Boisot (1995) refers to as 'information space' or 'C-space'.

Imaginary space

Those organizations with the best quality and density of imaginary space are those that can use and circulate knowledge most effectively. They have intelligent, well-trained and highly skilled employees who are good at imagining and creating and can work using metaphors, what Gareth Morgan (1993) has referred to the task of understanding and shaping organizations as 'imaginization'. They have the interpersonal and communicuations skills needed to conceptualize and circulate knowledge in the manner described by Senge (1990) in his model of the 'learning organization', and by Nonaka and Takeuchi (1995) in their 'hypertext organization'. The role of knowledge will be discussed in more detail in chapter 4. Here, it is important to note that successful acts of creativity or imagination depend on prior knowledge, which forms the basis of future action (Witzel 2000).

Imaginary space, however, is not unique to virtual organizations. Any successful organization has an imaginary space in which people do research, innovate new products, make strategy and ask 'what if' questions. To create a virtual organization, as with any business organization, the usual first step is to ask questions and find answers on a variety of subjects. Who are the organization's customers? What are their needs? What products and services can we produce, profitably, that will meet those needs? What kinds of employees, with what skills, will need to deliver those products? Who will provide the finance needed to make it all work? In this way, managers create a mental image of the organization, its purpose and its goals.

This step is the standard method of creating an organization as described in many textbooks, but Collins and Porras (1994) note that there is another way. Some successful businesses, they argue, begin with a team or a pool of knowledge, and only by analysing available resources do they eventually hit on a product and a market. They cite Hewlett-Packard as an example of a company that came together as a team based around two dominant US entrepreneurs, Bill Hewlett and David Packard, and then looked for a mission. Sony was founded under similar circumstances in post-war Japan around the team of Ibuka Masaru and Morita Akio.

However, this is still the same principle at work. Whether 'imagining' a market and a product and then putting together a team to make it, or creating a team and then determining how best to employ it, organization begins with an act of imagination. That initial act then goes on to sustain the organization, as managers and employees work to expand and/or amend the original space created. This is a truly creative, organic process; it cannot be done mechanistically. The bolder the imagining, the more original the outcome.

Then, and only then, does the organization go on to design itself, including the technology it needs to function effectively and the structure it requires to employ both its technological and HR. Just as structure follows strategy (Chandler 1962), so technology follows imagination.

Technology space

Just as with imaginary space, all organizations have a technology space of some sort, even if it is only a single telephone or computer in a tiny office. Technology space is the space created by the organization's technology networks (more will be said about these in chapter 3). It has two dimensions:

- the strength, breadth and durability of the networks themselves, including issues such as bandwidth, accessibility and reliability;
- the skill levels of the people using and maintaining the networks.

It is important to provide fit between these two elements. If the human operators lack the skills to get the most out of the network, then at best there is organizational potential – and investment – being wasted, and at worst unfamiliarity and poor usage will result in mistakes: garbage in, garbage out.

Technology space also has to fit with imaginary space. If the imaginary space is 'bigger' than the technology space, the latter will have to be upgraded. For example, having created the 'imaginary space' of a global distribution system, the corporation then must make sure its technology systems are capable of supporting it. But on the other hand, there is also a danger of the technology space becoming 'too big'. If the organization has more technology than it can use, then it has wasted investment. In 2002, newspapers such as the *Financial Times* and the *Wall Street Journal* published the results of a number of studies showing that IT investment by firms in the late 1990s has not yet been matched by corresponding returns in output or profitability; in many cases, such investments have yet to even pay for themselves. This may be jumping to conclusions too soon – it is possible that such investments will indeed pay for themselves over the longer term, and there may have been even greater costs incurred in not investing in IT – but nonetheless there is evidence that many firms invested in IT and other technologies on the grounds that their benefits could be taken for granted and without conducting a detailed cost/benefit analysis.

Cultural space

As noted above, an organization's culture creates its own space, which determines how knowledge flows and the types of knowledge that are most easily used. Cultural space represents the extent to which all members of the organization are able to occupy the same space and work effectively within it.

In order for cultural space to exist, there first has to be a fit between everyone's perception of the organization – that is, members of the organization have to share certain common values and, to at least some extent, view the organization in the same way. The organization's cultural space is not the sum of all its members' views and values; rather, it is the area where all those views and values converge. The more similarity there is between these views and values, the more dense the cultural space will be, as a greater number of people have 'bought into' the common organizational culture. In the words of Gareth Morgan, 'Organization always hinges on the creation of shared meanings and shared understandings, because there have to be common reference points if people are to shape an align their activities in an organized way' (Morgan 1986:11).

There are many different ways of looking at cultural space. For example, Hofstede (2001) characterizes culture as being made up of a mix of common values and common practices, and goes on to characterize cultures along a variety of dimensions: process-oriented vs results-oriented, professional vs parochial, open systems vs closed system, and so on. On another level, Boisot (1995) classifies cultures according to how they codify and diffuse knowledge. As Morgan (1986) rightly points out, all these various methods of looking at organization culture have their own validity, and it is probably best to use more than one method to examine each culture in order to gauge its attributes.

Just as it is important to ensure a fit between technology space and imaginary space, so it is equally important to create a fit between cultural space and technology space. In many ways, this is the most difficult and problematic aspect of virtual space: how to create a kind of 'shared imagination' in which people inhabit the same mental space and can work effectively in teams. The complexities, and perplexities, of this issue are much older than the idea of the virtual organization. Psychologists and epistemologists have for many centuries pondered on how and why people look at the same problem and come up with different solutions, and whether it is possible to change our thinking so that all members of a group think the same way. In *The Cream of the Jest* (1917), the American novelist James Branch Cabell created a device that would allow two people to share the same dream, even though they were unaware of each other's thoughts in waking life. The psychologist Edward Bernays (1928) argued not for technology, but for education and propaganda to ensure shared information and a common pattern of thought.

Decades further on, we are no closer to realizing either of those visions. One of the key problems is that of cognitive pluralism: in other words, two people experiencing the same set of phenomena will often perceive them in quite different ways. This is particularly so when people are under stress, such as during wartime. In *Day of Infamy*, a book based on hundreds of interviews with survivors of Pearl Harbour, the writer Walter Lord shows how two people standing a few feet from each other would perceive a violent event such as a falling bomb very differently; one would see the flash of the explosion but would not remember hearing the noise, the other would hear the bang and feel the blast but not remember the flash. Teamwork in such situations becomes difficult as well; in one recorded incident during the Battle of Britain, three RAF pilots simultaneously attacked a Luftwaffe bomber over Kent and all three later claimed to have shot it down; each of the three was entirely unaware of the presence of the other two in the same airspace.

And, of course, it is precisely under conditions of greatest stress that it is most important that a team work together, and to do that they must share the same cultural space, a space that is strong enough and vivid enough for all to buy into with the pressure of events driving perceptions in different directions. The armed forces try to overcome this by almost continuous training and rehearsal, preparing its members for action in stressful situations and at the same time reinforcing shared values and senses of mission. Something of this is replicated in ideas like the hypertext organization developed by Nonaka and Takeuchi (1995). The latter develop a fourfold methodology of knowledge dissemination – socialization, externalization, internalization and combination – each branch of which represents a series of techniques for bringing the knowledge of individuals together and diffusing it within the same cultural space.

Nonaka and Takeuchi's arguments show the importance of matching culture to technology and imagination. In order for a successful virtual space to be created, the individuals in the organization have to have three attributes:

- They must as individuals be capable of 'imagining' the organization both internally and externally within their own minds, keeping track of their own role and their relationships with others both inside and outside the organization.
- They must as individuals and as team members be able to manage and use sufficient levels of technology to maintain those relationships and manage their own knowledge.
- They must collectively share many of the same values and practices in order to ensure that relationships work as harmoniously as possible, and that the same concepts of knowledge, organization and culture prevail across the board.

If there is failure in any one of these areas, then the virtual space begins to break down. Insufficient imagination means workers and managers simply cannot comprehend the concept of what they are supposed to do, and become introspective or drop out altogether, meaning the networks of virtual space begin to fail. Insufficient technology means that people cannot get in touch with others in the networks, leading to frustration and the channelling or obstruction of knowledge flows. Insufficient cultural convergence means different ideas about the purpose of the organization prevail, leading again to network breakdown and even internal power blocs and feuding between groups struggling to make their own cultural values prevail.

The limits and extent of virtual space

The previous section noted how virtual space builds on three other concepts: the creative abilities of the organization, the technical capabilities of the organization, and the ability of the organization's members to work together as a team. Other factors may also serve to limit the extent of virtual space.

The span of control

The term 'span of control' refers to the ability of the manager to influence what is going on around him or her. In particular, it is often used to determine how many subordinate managers or workers should be assigned to each. If a manager has too many reports, then there is a danger that he or she will not be able to give the required level of attention to some, or all, of them. General Sir Ian Hamilton (1922), who is thought to have originated the term, thought that managers should have no more than eight, and preferably six, people reporting to them, and that the greater the geographic distance between managers and reports, the fewer reports there should be.

Virtual organization can, if employed correctly, render geography to a large extent irrelevant; subordinates can be in a different region, a different country or a different continent. However, co-ordination and supervision of employees and junior managers who are not in close proximity does require a somewhat different approach to management. Just one example will suffice: the futures trader Nick Leeson, working on the far side of the world from Barings Bank's head office in London, was able to elude supervision by his superiors and create a fraudulent series of trades that ultimately brought down the bank itself. At least part of the responsibility for this collapse lay with Barings' senior managers, who failed to set up an adequate supervisory system. Communication through cyberspace is not a substitute for auditing and accountability; subordinates in risky situations need still to be monitored.

The issue of numbers of subordinates remains much as it was. Control in virtual management requires the handling of a great deal of information and knowledge, usually more than in conventional organizations. This information and knowledge needs to be listened to, analysed and digested. When designing a virtual organization network, the number of nodes into which each manager is plugged needs to be carefully limited, if the manager is not to suffer from information overload.

The ability of systems to handle multiple users

This is both a human and a technological issue. Networks need to be designed to allow access to all members; on the other side of the coin, members of the network need the training and communications skills that will enable them to operate as a team, rather than relying on a single member, such as the network manager, to do all the co-ordination work.

A key issue here is the organizational 'asymmetry of power', first described by Friedrich von Hayek and discussed in more detail by Khalil (1996). This term refers to the fact that when we join organizations, such as businesses, we surrender a part of our autonomy to that business and agree to work in its best interests in exchange for reward (pay, fringe benefits etc.). We normally agree to do this because (a) the rewards outweigh the disadvantages of loss of autonomy, and (b) we share the organization's goals to at least some degree (few people are willing to work for long for organizations whose aims and methods they fundamentally disapprove of). Problems arise when the loss of autonomy is no longer compensated for by sufficient reward, or when we cease to share the organization's goals, or both.

Virtual networks have the capacity, if used correctly, simultaneously to reduce the loss of autonomy and increase shared values by enabling workers and managers to have more input and influence over how the network will function and what its goals will be. But this can only work if all have equal access to the network; otherwise, the asymmetry will remain and even become more pronounced. Two common problems in this area are:

- The tendency, noted above, to make networks more simple, whereas in fact functionality can only be increased by making them more complex; this means that access by some members to the network can be restricted.
- The tendency to assign gatekeeper roles to the network manager, rather than ensuring that the latter's main purpose is to facilitate equal access.

Knowledge resources

As we discuss in more detail below, an organization's virtual space is inevitably limited by its knowledge resources. In order to exploit the virtual space concept to the fullest, therefore, organizations need continually to acquire or create new knowledge. There is thus considerable overlap between the concept of the virtual organization and the learning organization/hypertext organization.

Put simply, organizations that are unable to learn effectively will find their virtual space to be heavily circumscribed. A constant flow and diffusion of knowledge is necessary in order to sustain virtual space. If no-one is transmitting knowledge along the network, then the whole comes to resemble a computer which has had its power switched off. Technology networks of even the most sophisticated design remain inert and lifeless until they are used. The organization must, therefore, be able to generate and/or acquire sufficient stocks of knowledge to keep its networks working.

Culture

The kind of culture an organization has dictates the nature of the knowledge it circulates and thus the shape of its virtual space. This issue is laid out in detail by Boisot (1995), and it is worth summarizing his views on the relationship between culture and knowledge in full.

Organizational knowledge, says Boisot, circulates in an organizational dimension which he calls 'C-space' (culture space). However, how it circulates and to what extent it does so depends on the type of knowledge. He begins by classifying knowledge along two dimensions: codification and diffusion. On the first dimension, codified knowledge is knowledge that can be easily set out and transmitted, while uncodified knowledge is more implicit and difficult to transmit. On the second dimension, diffused knowledge is that which is easily and readily shared, while undiffused knowledge is not readily shared. From this, the above author sets out a fourfold typology of knowledge:

- proprietary knowledge: codified but undiffused (easy to transmit but not widely shared);
- personal knowledge: uncodified and undiffused (not easy to transmit or share);
- public knowledge: codified and diffused (easy to transmit and widely shared);
- common sense: uncodified and diffused (not easy to transmit, yet widely shared).

Proprietary knowledge is often connected to specific things or artefacts which belong to a person or organization, and thus has an identifiable owner. It may well be written down or at least set out clearly, but the owners of the knowledge will often feel they have a vested interest in not sharing it, in order to protect their own position, power, competitive advantage etc. Personal knowledge, on the other hand, is very often locked up in our own minds, and is rarely codified in any form. This makes it hard to share with other people even if we want to; good communications skills (and, of course, a motive for sharing in the first place) are necessary.

Public knowledge is the easiest form of knowledge to acquire, as it is highly codified and widely available in books, newspapers, over the Internet or, if the original owners are feeling proactive and ready to share, through newsletters, meetings and briefings and other devices for communicating knowledge. Common sense is perhaps the most difficult area of knowledge to grapple with: it consists of a series of shared sets of knowledge and/or beliefs about certain subjects which remain highly uncodified. We all know it is foolish to stick our hand in a fire, yet fires do not contain large signs beside them saying 'Do not touch' (though if health and safety officials were to have their way, this probably would happen).

Having defined knowledge, Boisot now returns to culture. The organization's culture defines its cultural space, and the shape of C-space in turn makes some forms of knowledge dominant. Boisot says that the different kinds of knowledge are analogous to different forms of organizational culture, each of which privileges one kind of knowledge over the others. He calls his four forms markets, bureaucracies, fiefs and clans:

- Markets are cultures where public knowledge predominates. Knowledge has some of the attributes of a commodity, is well defined and is easily and frequently shared.

- Bureaucracies are cultures where proprietary knowledge predominates. Knowledge is codified, but the custodians of knowledge often adapt a protective attitude towards it, seeing their role as guardians of knowledge rather than as providers of it. Knowledge in these organizations is equated directly with power.

- Fiefs are cultures where personal knowledge predominates. Again, the guardians of knowledge tend to keep it close to themselves and do not share easily; but in addition, knowledge tends not to be codified. Organizations led by strong charismatic leaders who do not delegate and tend to give orders rather than explaining can be classed as fiefs.

- Clans are cultures where common-sense knowledge predominates. Knowledge tends not be recorded or transmitted formally, yet through informal channels everyone has access to the same knowledge and can draw on it.

Of these four types, bureaucracies and markets are of course the most common in business, as in most fields of human organization. Bureaucracies are dominated by the upper tiers of management, fiefs by a few strong leaders, but in both cases knowledge and power are concentrated at the top. The obvious route for breaking away from this has been the market model. To develop a market model of organization requires those at the top of the organization to surrender their custodianship of knowledge, and this means giving up power. Fiefs and clans are alternative models which are much less commonly found; the former tends to characterize entrepreneurial organizations, while the latter is found in some experimental radically decentralized organizations such Semco in Brazil (Semler 1993).

There are other ways of conceptualizing knowledge flows in organizations, but this model is particularly useful in showing how the organization's culture impacts on all three of the previous issues discussed. Its style of management dictates the span of control, and even more so, limits or enables access to key networks. It also determines how knowledge is created and used, and which types of knowledge will be considered most valuable and will be most commonly found. Culture, knowledge and organization structure can never be entirely separated from each other; each influences and determines the shape of the other two.

Management issues

Managing in virtual space requires a series of balances, which will be dictated in part by the culture of the organization, its knowledge resources and its span of control. Managers in virtual organizations face a constant series of tensions: how to empower employees to work more flexibly and more freely, but without letting them waste their efforts on work that may not be in the organization's own best interests and may not be helping to meet its goals. 'Flexibility and focus' is a paradox for virtual managers which they can only resolve by making a series of trade-offs and finding the best pragmatic solution. Choices have to be made along a series of sliding scales: co-ordination vs initiative, accountability vs empowerment, control vs flexibility, uncertainty vs planning, and group interests vs personal interests.

In some senses these trade-offs need to be made in conventional organizations as well, but the formless and abstract nature of virtual space makes the choices harder. In conventional organizations, it is comparatively easy to enforce centralized co-ordination, control and accountability, and assert the primacy of planning and group values. Centralized and concentrated physical locations mean the direct management of personal assets can be largely, or even entirely, about ensuring conformity. As we noted above, this style of management carries its own price in terms of rigidity, bureaucratization and so on, but the choice is there and available if this is the route down which senior managers wish to go. But this style of management is quite alien to the virtual organization, which indeed exists in the first place to overcome this kind of centralized rigidity. The question is, how far down each of these scales can the virtual manager go?

Co-ordination vs initiative

Working in virtual space requires people to use their initiative, rather than being told what to do. Even with real-time knowledge flows and communications, the dispersed nature of the organization requires people to take responsibility and act on their own for the good of the organization, rather than waiting for instructions. At the same time, what those individuals do must be in line with the organization's goals: the case of Barings Bank alluded to earlier, along with many similar cases, shows what happens when employees outside the organization's supervision and control begin to put their own interests first. Initiative has to be exercised within the overall framework of organizational goals; but how can this result be best achieved?

Accountability vs empowerment

Similarly, working in virtual space requires people to be empowered to act, yet at the same time they must be accountable for those actions. Where should the balance lie? As in any organization, too many procedures and too many rules restrict people's freedom of action, and encourage a play-it-safe mentality; if it is not in the rule book, then don't do it. This is to be avoided at all costs, but this does not mean that employees' activities should not be scrutinized, even over and above any regulatory and legal requirements. What combination provides the maximum of both empowerment and accountability?

Control vs flexibility

Moving on, working in virtual space requires flexibility and creativity, but it also requires control systems to measure performance and profitability. 'Control' is a 'dirty word' in management speak today, and we refer here not to 'controlling' workers themselves, but to controlling key factor inputs so as to ensure efficient and effective operations. In the boom years of the late 1990s, no-one worried much about efficiency, as it was thought that the only thing that mattered was results (for a discussion of the gradual disappearance of efficiency in terms of performance measurement see Breukel n.d.). yet the bottom line does matter, and in virtual organizations the problem of how to measure and define profitability becomes in many ways more problematic; how are virtual assets to be accounted for, for example (Warner and Witzel 1999)?

Uncertainty vs planning

Managing in virtual space requires people to be able to work in fuzzy situations and to manage paradox, but at the same time does not dispense with the need for planning and structure. If anything, these two fundamentals of business and management have become more important. During the late 1990s it was common to see the 'new' style of organization as transcending structure, and there was a widespread belief that changes in the business environment were moving too fast for planning. Wolff's now classic account of the dotcom boom, *Burn Rate* (1999), demonstrates graphically both the mindset of the time and the consequences of ignoring fundamentals. In fact, as Mintzberg (1989) had been arguing a decade before, concepts of strategy needed to change and are changing to include more fluid and *ad hoc* approaches. Similarly, the onset of new technology means that radical changes in structure now have become possible here as well (Warner and Witzel 1998; Franke 2002; see also chapter 3 below). But these are changes in degree, not in kind. Structures and strategy need, and evolve, to become more fluid and more flexible, but the need for them as generic concepts has not diminished.

Group vs personal

Finally, working in virtual space puts much more of a premium on personal qualities, yet individual employees and managers continue to need to be able to work together to ensure their group efforts are greater than the sum of their individual efforts. To do this requires a high degree of alignment between imagination space, technology space and cultural space, as discussed above. Only when people share the same values, vision and skills can teams work effectively across virtual space.

To sum up, we are back to the problem about encouraging people to dream the same dream, to share the same values and work in similar ways, all without sacrificing freedom, flexibility, initiative and creativity. Reinforce the value of culture; to be truly effective, a virtual space must also be a shared space. It follows that managing in virtual space is as much about managing culture as it is about technology. The HR department will find its role greatly magnified as it tries to find ways for people to buy into this shared space.

Conclusion

Much of the power and effectiveness of virtual organizations depends on how well they are initially designed and conceived. It is the alignment between three other spaces – imagination, technology and culture – that defines and creates virtual spaces. If the designers of the virtual organization can establish a good fit between these three, then the business can go well beyond its previous physical boundaries and into quite new realms of innovation and action. This is not to say that individual imagination and group culture cannot change: they can and do, and often technology is the imperative that forces them to do so. But technology unaided cannot achieve such change; it takes a strong and determined management to enable such changes and to ensure the ultimate fit between all three elements.

The potential of virtual space, in terms other than of freeing up resources and cutting costs, seems almost limitless. Yet, there are limits to virtual space, imposed by individual creative abilities, technical systems and group cultures. Virtual space is another kind of space, but some of the old constraints of organization still apply. And there are new dangers, of loss of focus and loss of control. The next two chapters look at how the deployment of a virtual organization's two primary technologies – its physical systems and its people – are essential to solving these problems.

Case Study *The virtualization of capital: the London International Financial Futures Exchange (LIFFE)*

By 1997, the London International Financial Futures Exchange (LIFFE) had risen to become the world's second largest financial derivatives market, eclipsing one established rival, the Chicago Mercantile Exchange, and challenging a second, the Chicago Board of Trade, for top spot. It had been helped to this position by London's rise to dominance of European financial markets. As LIFFE's own website puts it, 'London's markets are now the world centre of the euro financial markets, with around 45% all euro-denominated bond issuance conducted within the City, 32% of all global foreign exchange turnover, and 95% of all euro money market exchange-traded derivatives business'.

LIFFE's rise to prominence was accompanied by considerable debate both with the exchange's own management and with its major clients on whether to scrap the traditional outcry system and move to screen-based trading. In outcry systems, traders congregate, usually in a single venue, and tend to make

▶

deals on a face-to-face basis. Screen-based trading, such as had already been adopted in many other capital markets, means that trading is conducted from the trader's desk via computer and the Internet, without face-to-face contact. It means the scrapping of old-fashioned trading floors and the introduction of a virtual trading system.

Defenders of the the outcry system argued that it was faster and more responsive; traders could react instantly to changes in the market without the need to input data into a computer (in outcry systems, reconciliation always followed at a later stage, after the deal had been struck). Proponents of screen-based trading argued that technology could be used to speed up transactions, and that it would result in cost savings to investors.

Initially, the defenders of outcry won the day, one defender commenting that 'outcry has survived every innovation in history so far'. Within two years, however, LIFFE had reversed its position, as it began to see its business ebbing away to faster, cheaper, more flexible exchanges based on electronic trading. The trading floor and the outcry system were replaced by LIFFE CONNECT, the exchange's own bespoke system which allowed traders and investors to log on anywhere in the world. Significantly, 600 of LIFFE's 1000 employees were made redundant when LIFFE CONNECT was introduced.

The result has been the rejuvenation of LIFFE, which now trades capital – already a virtual commodity – in a virtual environment. The LIFFE CONNECT technology is the vehicle whereby vast quantities of virtual product are traded around the globe. That technology creates the framework which defines LIFFE's virtual space. The exact extent of that space depends on three factors:

- the guidelines for financial trading as laid down by UK law and the City of London's own regulations;
- LIFFE's own requirements for admitting new members; and
- the ability of new members to adapt to and use the LIFFE CONNECT software and system.

The first two factors are guided by the need to manage and control a sensitive industry and to maintain compliance with laws and regulations. The third is increasingly a matter of human skills and knowledge, as the technology itself is comparatively cheap and widely available. As the latter increases, LIFFE's membership and trading volumes both continue to grow.

Although the software that enables the space is highly sophisticated, the problems of imagination space and cultural space were equally complex. The requisite imagination space already existed on the part of some of LIFFE's members, many of whom also traded on other virtual exchanges and were used to conceptualizing themselves as part of such exchanges. Others, however, were not so far down the conceptual track and needed time to adjust. The same was true of many of LIFFE's own managers, who had not yet made the mental shift. Finally, the cultural paradigm within which LIFFE operated was strongly attached to the outcry system, which was a key part of the organization's conception of itself. This, too, needed to change, and the change required time. In the end, by adapting its own mental and cultural models to fit with the new technology, LIFFE was able to take advantage of the possibilities that technology offered.

Source: Patrick Young and Thomas Theys, *Capital Market Revolution: The Future of Markets in an Online World*, London, Financial Times/Prentice Hall, 2000; articles in the *Financial Times* and *The Economist*, passim.

3 Enabling virtual space through technology

Technology, as we have said in an earlier chapter, does not create virtual space, but it does enable it. What constitutes 'technology' is, of course, an open question, particularly given the rapid advances and changes in communications and data-storage technology that are going on around us. Rather than try to discuss the nature of technology or particular types of technology or its role in organizational behaviour, as we believe these topics are well covered already in the literature (see Loveridge 2001 for a good summary of this literature), therefore, we put forward a scheme for classifying technologies according to their function and purpose, and then show how these different classes can be combined to form different types of organization. It is important to note that, as spelled out in the previous chapter, the classes of technology adopted must also fit with the organization's broader strategic, organizational and cultural needs and imperatives.

This chapter discusses the use of technology in virtual organizations, discussing:

- the different types and classes of technology available;
- how these can be combined into technology systems; and
- the kinds of organizational options which can be had through the use of various technology mixes.

It will be immediately apparent that many, if not all, of the technology types and technology mixes discussed here also have application in 'conventional' organizations, and indeed we acknowledge this below. This should not come as any particular surprise. Technology represents a set of tools that, combined in different ways, enables different types of organization. What matters is not the technology itself, but the way it is combined and used along with the organization's human capital to create a virtual space. This is one of the themes of part III of this book.

When considering technology in relation to virtual organizations, the first emphasis is usually on communications technology. However, a number of other types of technology can also be used, including (but not limited to) information storage technology, monitoring technology, analytical technology and modelling technology, as well as older standard forms such as design, production and service delivery technologies. Which types are used and how they are employed will enable the business to function in the virtual space it has already designed and defined. Which types are selected for implementation and why is critical. This is new territory for speculation as to its impact on organizations and businesses, and we should be cautious in selecting the kinds of concepts we can use to understand the processes involved better (see Dunbar 2001).

The design of technological systems and the types adopted are of vital importance. Without adequate technological resources and investment, the organization will be unable to realize and/or fully exploit the virtual space it has designed. Suppose a business wishes to establish a virtual community with its key customers so as to provide them with regular updates on new products, changes in price and availability etc. The business may have adequate communications technologies to handle the customer contacts; but unless it also has adequate resources in terms of information storage, including databases of customer information and the means to link these to e-mail and other communications systems, then the goal will be difficult, even impossible to realize. Such systems are now available in standard or bespoke packages that can be set up with the aid of technicians and/or consultants, even for small to medium-sized enterprises (SMEs).

Technology is a necessary component of virtual organization; but it is not in itself sufficient. That is to say technology – some form of technology – becomes essential at any point when the organization is no longer concentrated in one place. As we pointed out in chapter 1, the simplest organization has a minimum level of technology. Every organization has a mix of factor inputs, labour and capital and even land, and there is a technological element to all of these. This has been true ever since the Industrial Revolution, if not before. Over time, though, technology has become more complex. Alfred Chandler (1962) has noted how the management of American railways, with operations often dispersed across several thousand miles, would have been virtually impossible without another new technology, the telegraph. The telegraph was also a critical component in the establishment of Reuters, the world's first news agency and a kind of proto-virtual organization (see the case study at the end of this chapter).

But, now as then, technology alone is not enough. Technology is basically a series of artefacts, which remain inert until set in motion by a human user or operator. The relationship between technology and its users, which is discussed in more detail in the following chapter, must never be forgotten when designing technology systems.

Classes of technology

The types of technology employed by virtual organizations are many and varied, but can be basically divided into the following classes.

Communications technology

Internet and, more recently, broadband communication technologies are at the heart of most virtual organizations. Intranets and other organization-specific technology forms are also important. Communications technology is most important in the circulation and dissemination of knowledge, which, as we shall discuss in a later chapter, is the lifeblood of the virtual organization. Communications links provide the web or network that link the various nodes of the organization and allow, first, contact, co-ordination and control to be maintained by head office, and second, remotely based employees to do their work and add value to the company's services and products. While there have been employees working at a distance – that is, remotely – in previous times, the proportion of such workers who can perform this task now gives operations a distinctive character.

Information storage technology

Information storage technologies such as databases and data archives are another essential feature of most virtual organizations. Data warehousing is now a very important business activity, in spite of the demise of many dotcoms. Data warehouses facilitate the storage of information and knowledge that have been created or acquired, and with these, the potential for future action. Knowledge becomes the main type of 'capital' of these firms. Virtual organizations, even more than conventional ones, require stocks of knowledge in order to function. Some operate mainly using knowledge as their main, or in some cases only, throughput. But even in more conventional businesses, the concept of the knowledge-intensive organization is now *de rigueur*.

Monitoring and scanning technology

Monitoring and scanning technologies scan the organization's environment for information that can be collected and assessed. Sometimes the purpose of these is security, such as CCTV systems that help to protect the organization and its assets from criminal damage. More commonly, this class includes data-gathering technologies such as EPOS (electronic point of sale) systems which gather data on sales volumes, average spend per customer, and so on.

These data-gathering technologies are especially important in setting up what are termed 'feedback loops', whereby knowledge that is gathered about organizational performance can be fed back into operations on an ongoing basis, resulting in a process of continuous improvement (Argyris and Schön 1978; Argyris 1993). In other words, they play a key part in helping organizations to learn by allowing them to scrutinize their own actions and learn from mistakes – and successes – as they happen rather than engaging in *post hoc* analysis. Using them in this way, however, requires a high level of managerial sophistication.

Analytical technology

Analytical technologies are those that can analyse a set of data and provide information in digestible form. They are an important interface between raw data (sets of numbers) and real information (facts and figures). Management information systems and variants on the type are an important example, allowing managers to interrogate stored data and analyse it for trends etc. Expert systems are common in many of the firms that use such technologies. These help their users to exploit the full potential of data available better.

Modelling technology

Still not yet widely used, modelling technology is sophisticated software that allows managers to create replicas of systems that can be studied and analysed, and variants created to study the alternative consequences of decision. Systems, such as virtual reality, are used in product and facilities design; more complex systems such as micro-worlds are used to study markets and economies and forecast future outcomes to situations. Modelling technologies have many uses, but one of the most common is to allow managers to replicate a variety of environmental and market scenarios.

Design technology

Design technology is a branch of modelling technology that allows initial product designs to be tested and analysed in virtual space before real prototypes are constructed. For example, aircraft designers who formerly had to rely on large and expensive wind tunnels to test new wing designs can now conduct many preliminary designs using computer models that will simulate airflows and other forces. Design technology is now very widespread in manufacturing industries. Additionally, systems design technologies are being employed to design everything from supply chains to service delivery systems.

Production technology

Production technologies are some of the oldest forms in use; for instance, the Venice Arsenal was an early form of the assembly line in the Renaissance, and Arkwright's factory system, dating from the late eighteenth century, was a basic form of modern production technology (see Fitton 1989). Today, such production technologies are increasingly moving into virtual space with robotically controlled systems, such as found for example at Fiat factories in Italy, Kawasaka plants in Japan or General Motors sites in North America, handling dangerous and hazardous work in particular. As much as a third of car-assembly work is currently handled by robots. Productivity has been boosted as a result of the use of such technologies, as well as product quality and reliability.

Service delivery technology

Service delivery technologies enable services to be delivered to customers through technology channels rather than face to face through human service staff (see Bateson 1995). These can be quite simple and not computer-based at all, like the conveyor belts that pass food items in front of customers in some sushi bars. More advanced systems include automatic teller machines (ATMs), the so-called 'hole in the wall' cash machines which, since their introduction in the early 1980s, have increasingly taken over from bank tellers as the main form of service delivery. Customers claim that they are more user-friendly than bank clerks. The Internet has enabled banks to deliver their services even more remotely, with online banking forming an early and important part of e-commerce. E-commerce has also been an important innovation, as in the case of airline ticket booking on the software provided by budget flight operators like Easyjet in the UK. Whether voicemail systems have been welcomed by the customer with as much enthusiasm is a moot point. Even if the dotcom collapse results in a slowing down of their expansion, many sites have survived and taken on new acquisitions even in the dark days of mid-2002, such as London-based travel agent lastminute.com. In the US, we have the examples of surviving online firms such as Amazon.com and ABE.com in the book retail industry, providing virtual sales systems for customers (and, in the case of ABE, booksellers) around the world.

Technology mixes for organizations

As noted, most virtual organizations rely on more than one class of technology. How these different types of technology are mixed and configured depends on the type of virtual organization that is required.

In fact, the issues is not usually as clear-cut as simply deciding what technology should be adopted. In practical and managerial terms, most technology exists in the form of systems, and these systems can be made up of one, two, three or even more technology types. In turn, most organizations – and nearly all virtual organizations – use a combination of various systems. Some examples of systems follow.

Communications systems

Simple communications systems are designed primarily for the exchange of information and the co-ordination of activity. They rely on communications technology, though some information storage technology may be required to hold and retain information beyond the capacity of an e-mail system on its own. Examples include academic discussion groups, e-journals and wire services, virtual learning networks and other 'systems within systems', as well as the now ubiquitous Internet and intranet e-mail systems. Many are multimedia, like Internet news sites such as those of the BBC or CNN, with screen pages, audio and video options. They are selected on a daily basis by millions of users.

Communications systems form part of all virtual organizations, but they are rarely the whole organization; other systems are needed if the network is to have anything to communicate. Internal links are also of major importance and intranets have become the norm in many organizations and especially elaborate in large firms.

Feedback systems

Feedback systems use a mix of monitoring and scanning technology and communications technology to gather information and pass it back to managers and decision-makers. They support the feedback loops which are essential on two levels: computerized production systems rely on servo-mechanical and other feedback systems to correct errors and maintain accuracy, while human feedback systems are important for learning and quality control. Again, these are systems within systems: a feedback system does not comprise an entire organization, though it is an important part of it. Examples include EPOS, mentioned above, and more sophisticated market intelligence systems that make market data available to managers.

Network systems

Network systems are a hybrid communications system onto which other technology types can be grafted according to the network's needs and functions. At a simple level, a communications system combined with a feedback system and with some analytical technology grafted on enables group analysis and decision-making; moreover, the members of the group do not have to be in physical proximity to each other. Management information systems and marketing information systems, for example, track stock flows and stock volume and sales figures and pass these on to all managers wherever they are, and the addition of analytical tools allows all managers in the network to analyse the data and discuss their conclusions. This system can in turn incorporate other types of technology: for example, links to production and service delivery technologies that are then incorporated into the network allows operations to be dispersed physically. Dispersed network systems dispense with physical concentration and aim to use communications technology as a substitute (albeit partial) for tangible structures such as office buildings etc. by enabling remote working, home working, tele-cottaging, and so on, a point to which we will return later. Increasingly, many retail banks are becoming dispersed systems with units such as credit centres, customer call centres, mortgage departments and so on spread around the country rather than being concentrated in one place. Virtual supply chains (see below) are also built up using network systems.

Service delivery systems

Service delivery systems are built, unsurprisingly, around service delivery technologies but they can also incorporate other technology types. Basic bank ATMs, for example, offer the delivery of a few limited services only, but more advanced ATMs now being introduced offer a limited two-way communication with the bank. At the other end of the scale, the service delivery systems adopted by the more successful dotcom companies, especially in the B2B arena, incorporate service delivery and communications technologies, information storage technologies to build up knowledge banks about each customer, and even modelling technologies that try to predict customer needs. Design and production technologies can be added to the system as required.

Knowledge management systems

Knowledge management systems combine information storage and analytical, modelling and communications technologies to facilitate the management of knowledge. The primary aim of most systems is to organize knowledge so as to make its rapid retrieval and use possible; in other words, to allow companies to exploit their knowledge capital more intensively (see chapter 5). One criticism of most knowledge management systems, however, is that they do not span the whole knowledge transformation process (see chapter 7): that is, they focus on knowledge organization or storage, and to a lesser extent on knowledge use, but fall down when it comes to knowledge creation. Nonaka and Takeuchi (1995) in particular have called for companies to be more aware of the need for knowledge creation and generation when establishing knowledge management systems.

Options for organizations

The existence and development of these various classes of technology and technology systems offers a number of new organizational options. Businesses are no longer dependent on concentration of capital; capital can now be dispersed and deployed in a variety of complex, often flexible and sometimes fuzzy organizational types. Some examples follow.

Dispersed organizations

The earliest form of virtual organization, the dispersed organization is a form which concentrates its capital in several different geographical locations rather than in one place. Banks and international trading companies were among the first to use this form, but the dispersed organization first had a major impact with the development of the railways. As Chandler (1977) has described in detail, railways, especially in America, operated over long distances, with staff, equipment and offices located hundreds or even thousands of miles apart. The organization was linked by the physical network of the railway track, but even so the railways could probably not have been managed efficiently without the invention of a new communications technology, the telegraph. The telegraph also enabled the emergence of dispersed organizations in other industries. Improved communications led to the growth of what Chandler describes as M-form or multidivisional firms such as Du Pont and General Motors. These firms divisionalized their operations so as to concentrate capital at many different points around the country; all linked the communications systems such as the telegraph and telephone.

Today, later generations of communications technology such as e-mail have made dispersed operations a norm for most companies of any size. Companies can now locate their capital – human and other – in the places where it is most needed and will be most effective, rather than being forced into geographical concentration in order to maintain control.

Virtual value chains

Virtual value chains are an extension of the dispersed organization concept based on a recognition that a product (or service) takes a journey from supplier of components to producer of the finished product and on to the consumer. Value is added not just by the producer but by a whole chain of organizations which have a common set of interests. From understanding the concept of the value chain, it is a short step to linking all the organizations in the value chain into a common system. Virtual supply chains are an increasingly common example of this. Virtual supply chains link suppliers, producers, distributors and retailers into a common communications network with feedback, monitoring and modelling technologies in order to achieve timely and efficient supply. Most large businesses in the automotive and consumer electronics sectors, for example, now use a form of virtual supply chain, although the concept is still undergoing development in practice (Schary and Skjøtt-Larsen 2001).

E-commerce

E-commerce became one of the business mantras of the late 1990s, and great things were expected of it. The bursting of the dotcom bubble in turn brought about widespread scepticism of e-commerce, but in fact, once the 1990s hyperbole is stripped away, the concept remains a very valuable and important one. E-commerce uses many of the communications technologies of the virtual value chain, but collapses the value chain to reduce the number of components in the chain to two or three at most. ABE.com, the online bookseller, plays a role as a middleman, introducing customers and suppliers of books to each other. It holds no stock of its own, and does not even necessarily handle cash; customers can place their orders through ABE, but they are also free to contact the bookseller directly and make their own arrangements for purchase. Other e-commerce organizations play more of a gatekeeper role and act as intermediaries between customers and suppliers in all cases.

Managing an e-commerce organization turned out to be much more complicated than their founders thought (we will come onto the reasons for this in part III of this book). But those that were well-managed from the beginning have survived and are beginning to turn profits, even if somewhat later than expected. E-Bay, the online auction house, is generally cited as one of the American dotcom success stories, and in Britain the travel and ticket retailer lastminute.com has defied its early critics and is now making healthy profits. E-commerce can be very successful, but success comes no more easily here than it does in any other organization.

Learning organizations

Not strictly classed as virtual organizations, learning organizations nevertheless have a strong virtual element. Multiple technologies are employed, including communications, information storage, feedback and analytical technologies to support the creation and diffusion of knowledge. Learning organizations are actually an organizational system; they are 'organizations that learn' rather than organizations whose primary function is learning, as the name might suggest. As Senge (1990) points out, learning organizations also have to be able to transmit their knowledge into value, and that brings in older technology classes such as design, production and service delivery. A fully functioning learning organization thus integrates a wide variety of technology forms in order to create a knowledge value chain. Examples of learning organizations are rare, but the World Bank's recent developments of an intensive global knowledge management system shows it to be moving in this direction (for more details on the World Bank see Dzinkowski 2002 and the case study at the end of chapter 5).

Hypertext organizations

The hypertext organization, first defined by Nonaka and Takeuchi (1995), is a more sophisticated form of learning organization, in which the organization is perceived as existing on several levels simultaneously. In particular, they describe this form of organization as a hybrid with 'a nonhierarchical self-organizing structure working in tandem with [the organization's] formal structure' (Nonaka and Takeuchi 1995:166). The ability to mix formal bureaucracies with informal and flexible taskforces or teams creates a multi-layered system in which individual project teams and the larger business system are both situated within, and depend upon, the organization's knowledge base. Their conception of how this works is worth quoting at length.

> The process of organizational knowledge creation is conceptualized as a dynamic cycle of knowledge traversing easily through the three layers [project team, business system and knowledge base]. Members of a project-team on the top layer, who are selected from diverse functions and departments across the business-system layer, engage in knowledge-creating activities … Once the team completes its task, members move down to the knowledge-base layer and make an inventory of the knowledge created and/or acquired during their time with the project team... After recategorizing and recontextualizing the new knowledge acquired, team members return to the business-system layer and engage in routine operations until they are called again for another project. The ability to switch among the different contexts of knowledge swiftly and flexibly, so as to form a dynamic cycle of knowledge, ultimately determines the organizational capability for innovation [Nonaka and Takeuchi 1995:169–70].

An examination of the hypertext organization concept shows it to be heavily dependent on supporting technology systems. In the first place, knowledge management systems are essential if knowledge is to be coded and categorized in the manner described. Second, communications systems are needed if project team members are to communicate not only with each other but with outside sources of knowledge. Finally, network systems would be seem to be natural technological analogue of the hypertext organization itself.

Virtual communities

Virtual communities are advanced forms of communications networks in which a number of different businesses or organizations take part on an ongoing basis. Virtual communities usually take one of two forms: research or other consortia formed to exchange information and knowledge, and marketing communities where a supplier is in regular contact with a small but related group of customers. Contact is frequent and two way. These can, for example, be found in supply chains. Manufacturers and retailers can also use virtual communities to obtain more accurate information about customer needs and wants. An example of the first type can be found in the virtual community established by the space agency NASA and its associated research centres to conduct research into space flight and associated issues, or the virtual research consortia set up between companies and/or universities. An example of the second type is the virtual community being established by the Bristol-based publisher Thoemmes Press and its key customers. The latter, a small group of librarians and academics, are kept informed by the publisher of future developments and frequently contribute ideas and suggestions for projects, which they may then be invited to edit or manage on behalf of the publisher. Communications and network systems are an essential component of this type of organization.

Virtual webs

The virtual web is, like the virtual value chain, a supra-organizational network, but rather than merely structuring organizations virtually along a particular value chain, it also spreads out to incorporate multiple organizations at the same stage of the chain. Franke (2002) defines the virtual web as a collaboration between partner firms with common interests. The concept has three components:

- The virtual web platform, 'a pool of independent companies that agree to co-operate. The virtual Web platform provides the environmental condition, such as trust and co-ordination mechanisms and tools, necessary for the dynamic configuration of market and customer-driven value-chain constellations' (Franke 2002:ii).

- The virtual corporation, 'temporary operational units that are configured on market opportunities/and or customer needs' and are established on a limited life basis by partner firms (Franke 2002:ii).

- The net-broker, a bespoke management organization 'that acts as inter-firm network facilitator. Basically, the net-broker initiates the virtual web plat-form, maintains the relationships between the web partner companies and facilitates the formation of market- and customer-driven temporary virtual corporations' (Franke 2002:ii).

Comparisons can be made between the hypertext organization, which acts within individual firms, and the virtual web, which sets up relationships between firms. Neither feels it necessary to dispense with conventional organizational forms; rather, these are seen as a platform from which flexible, limited-life task-forces or teams can be developed. In the latter case, the taskforce or team involves entire firms, not just groups of individuals. Limited-life consortia first began appearing in the late 1990s, primarily as partnerships between companies in research-intensive sectors such as electronics, biotechnology and defence systems. However, virtual webs do not necessarily have to be of limited duration; Airbus Industrie, a partnership between a number of European aviation companies, has some characteristics of a virtual web.

Hologram organizations

This is the most sophisticated form of all, in which, like a hologram, each component of the organization is a miniature replica of the whole. For example, each business unit, team etc. replicates on a smaller scale all the core functions of the entire organization. Defined by Morgan (1993), the hologram organization can be easily reconfigured and restructured, using technological networks as the physical 'backbone' of the organization while its other parts reconfigure to meet new demands. Some chain retailers in the US are now moving towards this form of organization. Whereas traditionally buying, supply, marketing, advertising and so on have been centralized functions, these are now being partially decentralized. A technology-based common supply chain exists, but local buyers are free to adopt a product mix that suits local customers; advertising, too, is becoming more localized, while head office concentrates on co-ordinating activities and on marketing the overall brand. Thus, local outlets operate within the overall parameters of the brand and the organization, but can reconfigure themselves in response to local market opportunities.

It should be noted that none of the above is ever in practice the sole form of organization adopted by a business. All organizations, even the most virtual such as online financial services providers, is in fact a hybrid of several virtual systems and conventional systems as well. Amazon.com may be the most widely quoted example of an e-commerce organization, but even it has offices and a warehouse. There is a need for a minimum of physical resource; even the leanest website may be linked, say, to the owner's home used as an office base. One of the strengths of Nonaka's hypertext model, quoted above, is that it allows the integration of both virtual and tangible systems, rather than assuming that one or the other must prevail.

Conclusion

To repeat, technology enables virtual space, but it does not define it. The latter is the task of the organization's people – especially its managers – who are responsible first for deciding the best organizational form for meeting the organization's goals, and then for choosing the right types of technology and combining them into the right systems in order to support that organization and enable its virtual space to become usable.

When choosing both organizational form and supporting technology, managers today are faced with a bewildering variety of options. There is no longer one 'best' form of organization, but a menu of types which can be examined, experimented with, and even combined in new hybrid types, all according to organizational requirements.

There is, of course, a further important aspect to the employment of technology. Technology is a series of artefacts; in order to create a virtual environment, or anything else, technology must be used. Virtual space is not created by technology; it is created by people using technology. When designing a virtual space and adopting supporting technologies, therefore, the fit between the organization's technology and its people is of first-water importance. The next chapter discusses the relationship between people and technology at work, and shows how old principles of technology management are still important for the virtual organization.

Case Study *Reuters*

In the 1840s, the telegraph was the Internet of its day, providing the ability to communicate with other people around Europe and, later, across the Atlantic, getting information in minutes that would formerly have taken days to transmit. In 1848, a newspaper editor in Paris, Charles Havas, experimented with setting up an agency that would provide details of events of the Paris Revolution of that year to foreign newspapers by telegraph. Havas failed to make money on the venture and soon abandoned it. However, one of his employees, a German emigré named Paul Julius Reuter, felt there was the prospect of making money by gathering and selling financial-market information over the telegraph network.

Reuter first established a small bureau in Aachen, Germany, and when this proved moderately successful, relocated to London in 1851, just as the first cable was being laid across the English Channel to connect London to the growing continental telegraph network. Reuter signed up the London Stock Exchange as his first client, providing news from continental exchanges, and followed this up with a growing list of brokerage houses and other business concerns both in London and on the Continent. Under Reuter's system, there were no preferred clients: every customer joined the same network, which Reuter himself managed from his London office through agents around Europe, and all received the same information at the same time.

The rapid growth of this service led Reuter to expand into political news, and he soon signed up *The Times* and other major London newspapers, followed by provincial British papers and then newspapers and journals on the Continent.

▶

During the Franco–Austrian war of 1859, Reuter's correspondents provided information straight from the battlefield, which was telegraphed around Europe in a few hours and appeared in newspapers the next day. The electrifying impact of this development was much like that of the broadcast of the first live-action films of the Gulf War by satellite television relays in 1990–1; the ability to bring the news across the continent and into people's homes quickly and accurately made Reuter's reputation and led to the founding of an entire new industry. Reuter's vision of how communications networks function was the starting point for the modern global media empires of today.

Reuter showed how it is possible to expand the scope of operations by using technology to create a virtual space. Reuters was not – and still is not – a concentrated organization; it exists as a series of network lines and nodes, all emanating out of the London headquarters. Later news agencies developed new technologies – radio, television, satellite communications, the Internet – and have successfully challenged the position of Reuters as the world's leading news agency. However, it is worth noting that all have used the same funda mental model: dispersed news-gathering operations which transmit data through a central network focus and then on to clients.

Source: D. Read (1992), *The Power of News: The History of Reuters, 1899–1989*, Oxford: Oxford University Press.

4 Ghosts in the machine: how people work in virtual space

The problem of finding the right balance between people and technology has been a problem for management – and for society more generally – ever since the Industrial Revolution. Then, groups such as the Luddites, the machine-breakers of that epoch in England, fearing that technology would put them out of work, destroyed machinery and campaigned for a return to 'hand-work' in trades such as textiles, in particular. Subsequently, explosive growth in mechanical, then electrical and most recently electronic technology has changed the nature of work in almost every industry.

Whether what we are seeing now is a second, or third Industrial Revolution depends on the periodization and interpretation one adopts. We would certainly see it as a 'post-modern' development that bridges the last and present millennia. Technological changes now ongoing may be leading to a quantum leap in business communication that offer significant changes in work organization.

Commentators have seen both positive and negative sides to this growth and change. On the one hand, the advance of technology has made individual workers more productive and, in the vast majority of cases, more prosperous personally. On the other hand, technology has brought with a great expansion vis-à-vis top management's powers of control. All technology is open to abuse, and the abuse of communications technology in particular can be seen in organizations where communication is directive and top-down only, where employee communications are monitored, and where tight procedures are enforced with little freedom of individual action.

Two twentieth-century writers, both North American, epitomize these alternative points of view. The Canadian 'media guru' and scholar Marshall McLuhan (1962) argues that the advance of technology, particularly communications technology, was more or less a return to a golden age when communication was free and was not circumscribed by the boundaries of print. He foresees the new advances as being a global leveller, smoothing out differences between people and cultures and bringing new understanding and harmony. On the other hand, Lewis Mumford (1967), an American polymath, sees the dangers of technology becoming a dominant tool in the hands of a capitalist upper class, used to control and manipulate the every action of workers inside what he called the 'megatechnic wasteland'. Mumford's views are reminiscent of the utilitarian thinker Jeremy Bentham in nineteenth-century Britain, whose concept of a 'panopticon', a prison model in which total surveillance was possible, was taken up later in the last century by authors in France like the post-modernist Michel Foucault (1975).

Technology has changed much, but it has not transformed everything. Despite the advances made by technology and the changing nature of work, organizations continue to be staffed and run by people. The idea of a 'peopleless' organization may be intriguing, but it will rarely if ever be practical – not, at least, until artificial intelligence systems have advanced by several orders of magnitude beyond their current state of development. The main barrier to the idea of the peopleless organization is that people remain the prime generators and users of knowledge, and therefore cannot be dispensed with. They are, for example, the holders of 'tacit knowledge'. Without them, an organization is inert; indeed, without people it is questionable whether an organization can be said to exist at all.

The problem that besets almost every business, especially those of a certain size, is how to strike the right balance between technology and human systems, between enabling people to work to their full potential and controlling or co-ordinating their actions for the good of the corporation. Experiments with organizations have a long pedigree, having progressed by trial and error along an evolutionary path towards adaptation and differentiation (see Warner 1984).

In the 1980s and early 1990s, particularly in North America, books such as Tom Peters's *Thriving on Chaos* (1987) and *Liberation Management* (1992) urged the breaking down of all systems to enable employees to create. But most US and British corporations remained conventional in their organization and corporate ethos. There have always been deviant examples of firms that managed differently, but they were the exceptions. In the field of self-management, odd examples in both North America and Europe were often cited as 'different'; indeed for a time even national systems like that of the former Yugoslavia implemented such self-management policies.

In Brazil, Ricardo Semler (1993) at his company, Semco, seemed to have created a near-perfect 'chaos organization' with no job descriptions, no formal discipline or set working hours and no internal borders. Yet, rare examples like Semco aside, it is usually the case that the members of an organization cannot all be simply turned loose to do as they please. Without some form of direction or co-ordination, much of their efforts will be dissipated into directions that do not serve the organization's aims and are thus, from the business perspective, wasted. Some of these efforts may be downright harmful, whether intended so deliberately or otherwise. Therefore, some form of direction or guidance is always necessary, whether it be self-imposed – as in the case of Semco – or, more commonly, issuing from senior managers and leaders. Warner and Witzel (1998) suggest that this direction and co-ordination is one of the main tasks of the general manager, and this idea will be discussed in more detail in part III below.

The age of top-down directive control, after the fashion of an army unit or a feudal fief, may be passing – though not quite so quickly as some might think – but this has not meant that control of every sort can be dispensed with altogether. The need for direction is a given in this formulation. How this direction and co-ordination is brought about, however, depends on the nature of the organization and its culture. Nowhere is this more important in virtual organizations, which as we noted in chapter 2 involve a series of trade-offs between freedom and co-ordination and involve a – possibly reduced – asymmetry of power. How these trade-offs are managed depends in part on the organization's culture and in part on its technology resources. Clearly, arriving at a new balance between the two above values is the managerial challenge of the new millennium.

As a very general rule, it can be said that virtual organizations have the potential to offer more freedom and creativity without loss of co-ordination and direction, and can thus potentially reduce the asymmetry of power. But to achieve this benefit requires very careful management indeed. Err too far in one direction, and the organization becomes loose and unco-ordinated, with employees working outside the organization's span of control and becoming unaccountable. Too far in the other direction, and the organization becomes as tight and restrictive and inflexible as the conventional organization it was supposed to replace. Virtual organizations may create greater employee 'empowerment' in some cases (as for example they do in software development) but restrict autonomy in others (as in the case of 'call centres').

The organization's needs, for flexibility and creativity but also accountability and focus, have to be carefully balanced, but so too do the needs and habits and culture of its employees. In order to do this, we need to look hard at how virtual organization changes work. What, in a virtual organization, is a job? Where, how and when should it be performed? What is most important, the process or the end result? This latter is not as easy a question as it sounds; in some sectors, such as finance and law, process really does matter, for regulatory and legal reasons if nothing else. And increasingly in other sectors, too, social and ethical pressures mean managers must be seen to be achieving the right results and doing so in acceptable ways. In a world after Enron – and Global Crossing, and Tyco and WorldCom etc. – managers must not only do the right thing but they must be seen to be doing it in the right manner. Transparency, then, is an important component of any virtual organization.

Human motivation is also important. Why do people work, and if they are working, why should they prefer to work in a virtual organization rather than a conventional one? Richard Donkin (2001:328) notes how new technology is changing the face of work so that:

> Our identities will no longer be framed by a single source of income or a single employer. They may be defined partially by a skill or set of skills or changing skills as we adapt throughout life; they may be defined by our values, and they may be defined by our circumstances. But in future our world will no longer be dominated by virtuous work. We have become conditioned to the idea of living for work. But the changing workplace, gradually undergoing transformation through the forces of flexibility, teleworking, home working and work/life balance, aided by constantly improving remote communications, is influencing a change in attitudes, and the job opportunities today seem greater than they have ever been before.

Yet the same author also notes that while technology offers people the opportunity to repackage their work in ways that suit them, in practice it seldom works out that way. Even as the old work ethic of 'virtuous work' is disappearing, people working virtually tend to work longer hours and have higher stress levels, with less time for leisure. And the new method of work will not benefit all the workforce. More than a decade ago, one British management pundit, Charles Handy, in his theory of the 'shamrock' organization (Handy 1989) warned against the dangers of the rising numbers of temporary and transient workers becoming a kind of perpetual underclass, poorly paid and poorly treated by employers who dispense with their services when no longer needed. Today, there is little doubt that increased flexibility in labour markets and employment practices have eroded job security. Further, there are increasing signs that much of virtual work is falling into this category, as the pay and conditions for workers in many call centres amply demonstrate.

So, there would appear to be advantages and disadvantages to virtual working. In broad, general terms, then, will the virtual organization make working conditions better, or worse? Will the benefits outweigh the disadvantages, or vice versa? Much lies in personal perception, and the kinds of personal needs for and satisfaction derived from work that Donkin (2001) discusses. Some employees will see the opportunities and jump at them. Others, motivated by fear for their personal security or simply innate conservatism, will prefer not to risk any changes in their way of working, preferring the devil they know. It may seem illogical to fight to preserve a way of working that is unpleasant or unfulfilling, as in the extreme case of the British coal miners striking in the 1980s to preserve jobs that were dirty, unhealthy and often dangerous; but as Donkin remarks, many people live for work, and any change in working patterns and routines becomes a threat. One of the greatest risks in setting up a virtual organization is that existing employees – who may be highly valuable in terms of their existing skills and knowledge – may refuse to buy into the new model and resist its implementation. Where there is uncertainty, employees will be cautious, even suspicious, setting up the kind of 'defensive routines' discussed by Argyris (1971) to block change and preserve the organization as they know it.

People and knowledge in virtual space

We are all familiar with the saying 'an organization is only as good as its people' (there are many variants); indeed, this is even truer of virtual organizations. One of the paradoxes of virtual organization is that the higher the levels of technology, the more important the role of human agency becomes. Virtual organizations depend utterly on people, without whom their systems and technology would only be lifeless artefacts. It is this scarcity of key employees that has led to rising rewards for the few and relatively weaker rewards for the others.

The importance of people in the virtual organization centres on their roles as producers, transmitters and users of knowledge. More will be said on the relationship between knowledge capital and human capital in chapter 5. For the moment, it is important to recognize that knowledge is inseparable from agency. For anything to be known, there must be a 'knower'. Only a knower can have prior knowledge; only a knower can be conscious and aware, and only a knower can combine these two to apprehend data and understand information (Witzel 2000). There are, of course, arguments about when an entity is capable of knowing. Do horses 'know' in the same way that we do? Are single-cell life forms such as amoeba capable of 'knowing'? These are interesting questions, but as there are very few horses in management (and even fewer amoeba), they can probably be left behind. The main point on which nearly all philosophies of knowledge are agreed is that, even if, as in the case of the Indian concept of *pramana*, there are sources of knowledge that exist separate from us, some sort of active agency is nonetheless required for knowledge to be apprehended and used. Critically, this active agency can be either individual human beings or groups of people, such as organizations and businesses.

It is important also to note the interdependence of consciousness and agency. Only agents are capable of consciousness; computers, for example are not. Second, given that knowledge is dependent on both consciousness and agency, it follows that only conscious agents can use knowledge to acquire further knowledge. Finally, given the separation of knowledge and fact, it follows that only conscious agents in possession of contingent knowledge can apprehend facts and understand information, both prerequisite activities to creating or learning further knowledge.

What does this mean in practical terms? First of all, knowledge is solely a function of the human brain. Neuroscience has even discovered that memory, the part of the brain that holds knowledge actually has two component parts: one that holds stored knowledge, and another that uses and manages it as and when required. Computers are now routinely employed to store and even to use knowledge on our behalf. However, lacking consciousness and there-fore agency, they cannot do so independently; lacking both of these, they cannot form independent judgements (they can form limited judgements based on probabilities, but these are always dependent on parameters preset by their programmers). Computers are also unaffected by cognitive pluralism, the phenomena whereby two people perceiving the same set of data will sometimes draw different conclusions from them (as described in chapter 2 above). Two computers, asked to analyse the same set of data, will always – bar malfunction – give the same result. Finally, as Greenfield (1997) points out, computers are only capable of apprehending data empirically, as it is provided by their input devices; they have no capacity of intuition. It is for this reason that Strassman (1990) remarked that a computer's value on its own is only what it will fetch at auction. It is up to managers to use the computer as a tool to add value to the businesses they manage. It is the information that a computer can process, not the artefact itself, that renders it useful.

Knowledge can be stored passively, in the human memory or in artefacts. These latter can be simple (such as symbols or signs; Boisot's [1995] traffic light is an example) or complex, such as printed books, film or computer memories. There is a spectrum of these symbols and signs, ranging from the minimal to the maximal in terms of information incorporated in them. The purpose of knowledge, however, is to function at the behest of an active agency; knowledge only becomes 'useful' when it is employed by such an agent. We define 'useful' here as knowledge which is capable of adding value, by directly improving a product or service offered to customers, by helping to create a new product or service to satisfy customer needs, or by improving and making more efficient/effective the processes by which the organization functions and products and services are designed and delivered. These are functions of knowledge which have a bottom-line impact on management performance, and in the end it is according to these criteria that knowledge must be measured and valued (see chapter 6).

Is there then any distinction between knowledge and action? Zeleny (2000:4–5) has described what might be called a 'process theory of knowledge' and argues that knowledge cannot be separated from doing. However, although the possession of knowledge by agents suggests that they may be intrinsically linked, a difference does nonetheless need to be drawn. First, it is possible to conceive of action without knowledge: belief or guesswork may lead us to undertake an action even though we have no knowledge of its consequences or our own desire to undertake the action. Second, it is also possible to conceive of knowledge without action. Such knowledge would effectively be in storage, in memory or coded into artefacts, symbols and language, waiting to be activated. Such imaginings of knowledge do not constitute activity by that knowledge; we can image the British Library, but we may not be aware of all the knowledge that is stored in it.

This may seem like hair-splitting, but it is important to get right the relationship between knowledge and agency, the critical point on which our final definition must turn. The Austrian-born but US-based management guru *par excellence*, Peter Drucker (1989:242) acknowledges this when he defines knowledge as that which 'changes something or somebody – either by becoming grounds for action, or by making an individual (or an institution) capable of different and more effective action'. Our definition here is simpler: knowledge is the stored prerequisite for action. Our brains are constantly engaged in what we can call a 'knowledge management cycle', apprehending data, retrieving stored knowledge so as to understand the information presented to us, understanding the require-ments of the situation, and taking appropriate action. Without knowledge, action becomes impossible. In the virtual organizational world, virtual knowledge becomes the common currency (Witzel 2000).

This brings us full circle to the notion that the virtual organization is even more dependent on people than is the conventional form of organization. The knowledge quotient of virtual organizations is higher – they require more knowledge and they use it more frequently – and therefore they need active human agency to create and circulate knowledge and manage the artefacts (information storage systems and so forth) where it rests when not in use. The human agency provides the appropriate factor input, namely human capital (see chapter 5). Put simply, there is no substitute for people in virtual organization.

The nature of virtual work

Knowledge is of course used in conventional organizations. But when we say that virtual organizations are more dependent on knowledge, what we mean is that in order to work virtually, employees require more knowledge and of different types. One of the great advantages of conventional organizations is that they allow for very intense specialization: an employee can be rigorously trained in a single minute task, or handful of tasks, and be expected to perform it or them to perfection every time. Virtual work is more diffused, less specialized and more 'fuzzy'. It is here that the virtual organization parts company from Taylorism and the functional division of labour. Employees in this context need to perform a variety of tasks, and very often need to structure the environment and systems they use to perform their tasks. The following are some of the key features of virtual working:

- Virtual working is less specialized and less functional. There is much less division of labour, and workers typically undertake a greater variety of tasks associated with a specific project. There is also more task-sharing. Some functional tasks can be automated; others are bundled together with other tasks to form larger projects. Rather than work solely on a specific task connected to a project, virtual workers are more likely to work on a series of tasks or even an entire project in all its aspects, according to the taskforce model described by Nonaka and Takeuchi (1995).

- Virtual work is more managerial. Virtual workers spend more of their time on tasks that would formerly have been considered 'white collar' or managerial, to the point where the distinction between white-collar and blue-collar work becomes blurred. This happens partly as a result of the lesser division of labour and lower levels of specialization noted above; workers must in effect become their own managers, co-ordinating their own efforts on a variety of tasks. Also, when working remotely, workers have to structure their own time and create their own working environment: it is up to them to decide how and when tasks get done, and often to set their own performance targets.

- Virtual work requires a greater variety of skills, including more soft skills. It follows from the previous two points that virtual workers require more general skills, to enable them to perform a number of tasks. Breadth of skill base becomes as important, if not more so, than depth. There is also an emphasis on soft skills such as communications and networking. This is a change in degree rather than kind from conventional organizations, where these skills are also important: when working remotely, for example, the emphasis in communications is not so much in face-to-face communication (interpreting body language and so on) but in interpreting signals received over media such as the telephone and e-mail. The rise of e-mail has renewed the importance for managers to have good written communications skills, skills that had been in danger of being lost in the previous technological era when the telephone was the dominant means of communication.

- Virtual work is more personalized. Workers can adapt their own working methods to the work required, and vice versa. Work-spaces can be personalized and made to seem more 'homely', even if the worker is not actually working at home. In many cases, hours can be adapted to suit the worker's own choice and needs, perhaps to allow him or her more leisure time or time with family. Also, because workers are less specialized, they tend to 'own' more of each project on which they work, and there is a tendency for them to identify more strongly with their work. Paradoxically, this identification with work can lead to longer hours and higher stress unless managed carefully. Virtual management may operate round the clock, by its very nature; time, like space, is no longer a constraint.

- Virtual work requires more personal responsibility. Virtual working often means less direct supervision. The corollary of this is that it is up to workers themselves to ensure that they meet performance targets, do quality work and carry out their work in a responsible manner that is consistent with industry and local regulations and the organization's own code of ethics. On the opposite side of the coin, workers need to manage their own lives and careers so that they achieve their goals while avoiding overwork and stress. Again, this departs from conventional Taylorist management and moves towards a new paradigm of work.

- Virtual work requires higher levels of motivation. Conventional organizations can rely to some extent on a group-work ethic or team ethic to provide motivation. The human need for socialization, discussed in detail by Abraham Maslow (1954), an influential writer on motivation, as part of the hierarchy of needs, provides an additional motivating force over and above the need to earn an income to provide food, shelter and security. In most virtual organizations, socialization is much more difficult to provide. Group values are more difficult to transmit virtually; a person who wishes to opt out of the group needs merely turn off his or her computer. There are ways of socializing virtual organizations, but managers need also to look at the highest level of the hierarchy of needs, self-actualization, and find ways of motivating people through self-fulfilment (see also below).

- Virtual work is less task-oriented and more result-oriented. This is an inevitable aspect of remote working. Some authors have compared virtual organization to a return to the craft working before the Industrial Revolution, when producers contracted out jobs and paid piecework rates for work completed. This form of work has its advantages in terms of being less management-intensive. However, it can result in higher transaction costs. Also, as Langlois (1999) has pointed out, contracting out leaves responsibility for quality down to the individual worker; the producing organization can only inspect quality at the end of the process, and has little or no ability to build quality in at the start. This need not necessarily be the case in virtual organizations, provided workers are trained and motivated to achieve quality, but, as noted above, quality becomes one of the worker's personal managerial responsibilities. Here, we can conceptualize a form of 'virtual quality management', or VQM, which becomes part of the virtual management task: top – or central – management will have responsibility for setting quality standards and providing tools to enable workers to meet those standards, but responsibility for meeting standards will devolve to the individual.

Motivation, co-ordination and accountability

As the above has shown, virtual working raises three important managerial problems: how to maintain worker motivation, how to achieve co-ordination and focus and how to ensure accountability. These should not be treated as three separate problems; they are all to a degree interrelated. In particular, motivation should be seen as the prerequisite for the other two. Workers who are sufficiently motivated will work harder to achieve the organization's goals, and will be more likely to be accountable and to behave 'correctly'. We set out the implications of this below.

Motivation

One of the most important aspects of virtual organization is the need to rethink the relationship between people as individuals and organization. As noted above, organizations exert an influence over their members that can help to motivate – or demotivate – them. There is a need for a motivational dynamic to activate the work process.

Reference was made above to the concept of the hierarchy of needs, first developed by Maslow (1954). This concept provides a very useful way of approaching the issue of motivation in the workplace. Summarizing very briefly, Maslow believes that human behaviour is motivated by the desire to fulfil certain needs, and goes on to classify these needs in a fivefold ascending hierarchy. The three lowest levels of the hierarchy are the need for food, the need for shelter and the need for socialization or belonging – the need to belong to and be part of a society of others. The two higher-order needs are the need for self-esteem, so that we ourselves place value on ourselves, and finally the need for self-actualization or self-fulfilment, so that we feel we are doing something of lasting value or worth.

Work fulfils the first two needs by providing money, which can be used to buy food and buy or rent accommodation. But, as Donkin (2001) points out, it also fulfils the need for socialization. This need is easily fulfilled in conventional organizations, where people rub shoulders with each other on an ongoing basis in the office or on the shop floor. In virtual organizations, though, the problem of socialization becomes much more difficult. When people work in physical isolation from each other, they tend to feel lonely and cut off; the socialization need is no longer being fulfilled. People need to mix together and it is sometimes said that the 'long-hours culture' is undermining the cohesion of many firms these days, as there is less time to meet colleagues for coffee at work or a drink after work, or to take part in sports.

That socialization is important is shown by the case of investment bank Merrill Lynch, following the terrorist attacks of 11 September 2001, when its office building in Manhattan had to be evacuated. Although several temporary premises were found in New Jersey, these were not large enough to accommodate all of the New York office staff, and many hundreds of these were asked to work from home. For these home-workers, the loss of socialization and contact with their colleagues was a major additional source of stress. Merrill Lynch responded by setting up a series of systems for keeping employees in contact with each other and head office, including a daily newsletter to tell the home-workers what was happening downtown, both with the company and in New York more generally in the aftermath of the disaster.

This does not mean that in the virtual organization socialization can never occur. But it takes more effort to ensure that people do socialize, and managers need to innovate new methods of socialization that will fit with their own organizational structure and their people's needs. Too often, virtual organization is seen as appealing to still higher-order needs, for self-esteem and self-fulfilment; the freedom and independence of virtual organization, it is offered, give people more control, so that they feel better about themselves and about their work. But according to the hierarchy of needs, higher-order needs cannot be fully satisfied until lower-order needs have first been fulfilled. In other words, socialization must precede self-esteem. The manager of the virtual organization must consider this when working out how to motivate his or her subordinates.

Co-ordination

As we have noted above, one of the key problems in a virtual organization is ensuring the right degree of co-ordination: enough to keep focused on the organization's goals, but not too much to restrict creativity and flexibility. There are in effect three methods of ensuring co-ordination:

- 'top-down', as in the line and staff method;
- 'centre-outwards', the network method;
- 'diffused co-ordination', the reciprocal method.

Top-down, or line and staff, co-ordination is often seen as the easiest form to implement, but it is at the same time the most restrictive, being generally associated with control rather than co-ordination *per se*. Central co-ordination is the form often advocated with network businesses, such as virtual organizations often are. Although less hierarchical, this kind of co-ordination can, if improperly handled, become equally restrictive. There is a tendency for the centre of co-ordination to gravitate towards the centre of power; that is, co-ordination can become the province of network brokers or other key nodes such as the main sources of information and knowledge. This can have quite unintended consequences.

The term 'reciprocal co-ordination' derives from the classical 'human relations' guru writing in the 1920s and early 1930s, Mary Parker Follett (Follett 1937), whose reputation has recently been revived; echoes of it can also be seen in Gareth Morgan's concept of the hologram organization, described above. Follett saw co-ordination as being a continuous process of 'adjustment' to the needs of other members of the organization. When two or more people work together, she says, they combine their thinking through 'adjustment'. In a game of doubles tennis, for example, each player has to adjust their thinking to take account of the movements and actions of their partner. In a large business organization, the heads of each department constantly 'adjust' their thinking to reflect the actions and activities of their colleagues and their departments. This adjustment is reflected in the way in which each head controls his or her own department. At the same time, of course, they are also adjusting their thinking to a whole host of other factors in the environment around them. All these different sets of thinking interpenetrate each other, and the activities of any one department reflect this combined thinking set that governs its co-ordination. Thus, no department exists in isolation, nor is the organization merely a set of departments set side by side: rather, it is a unified whole bound together by this set of dynamic, constantly changing relationships. This in turn affects everything that the organization and its members do.

Reciprocal co-ordination is by far and away the most effective form of co-ordination. It can be seen in the work of highly trained army units such as the SAS or the commandos, whose members know their own roles, the roles of their colleagues and how to adapt their own actions to meet changing circumstances all without losing focus on the final goal. Top-level football and rugby teams exhibit the same characteristics. Semi-autonomous work teams often exemplify these traits, as the work of the London-based 'Tavistock Institute' school (see Warner 1984) has shown. But, as these examples show, reciprocal co-ordination only works when all members of the organization are highly trained and highly motivated, with a flat organizational structure.

Accountability

Again as noted above, there is a strong need for transparency in virtual organizations. In the modern business environment, especially in the wake of the collapse of Enron in 2002, the pressure is on for business organizations of all types to become more accountable and to behave more ethically if they are to avoid crippling government regulations aimed at enforcing compliance. And, as the cases of not only British-based Barings Bank but also the Japanese multinational Sumitomo and, more recently, Allied Irish Bank show, compliance becomes much more difficult to enforce in organizations where key employees work at a distance from headquarters.

To counteract this, virtual organizations need strong codes of ethics that emphasize transparency, accountability and social responsibility. As compliance cannot be enforced, workers need instead to be motivated to act in ways that are best for the company, as well as themselves. Induction, socialization and training can also help in this regard, as employees need to internalize the recommended norms of the firm and buy into its system of ethics and values.

CESTA: the relationship between people and technology

The balance between people and technology in a virtual organization requires that the technology provide a system which enables work to be done Creatively, Easily, to a high Standard, in a Timely fashion and Accountably.

- Creatively: technology must facilitate working in creative ways, and must be capable of adapting as new innovations expand work and product parameters. If technology inhibits creativity, then two things will happen: the value the organization can add will be limited, and its capital will no longer be delivering on its full potential, and employees will feel inhibited and develop a sense of frustration derived from knowing that 'more could be done', but 'the system won't let me'. The need to enable employees to act creatively is urged by Peters and Waterman (1982) and, with some qualifications, has been repeated by nearly every major management writer since.

- Easily: technology must make communications, knowledge management and other forms of working seem easier than they were before, not harder. There is a paradox here: as noted previously, the work of cyberneticists such as Kolmogorov (1965) suggests that in order to become more inclusive, technical systems have to become more complex. Thus a system which makes work 'easy' will often itself be very complex in terms of design and maintenance. This in turn suggests that technological systems do not necessarily reduce the amount of capital employed, but rather require a shift in the way capital is deployed, with more effort devoted to designing and maintaining systems which then require less effort to use. Regardless of this, employees presented with a technical system which renders their work more difficult or complex are likely to develop defensive routines against that technology.

- Standards: quality still matters in the virtual organization, as many dotcoms found to their own cost. The difference is that the actual measurement and monitoring of quality is now very often the province of the individual worker. Technology systems need not only to help build in quality from the beginning of each work process, but they need also to enable workers to easily check and monitor the quality of their own work. Ideally, in this kind of 'virtual quality management', quality tasks should be designed so that they are seen as part of the individual's workflow, rather than a separate set of tasks that detract from the main effort. Many teachers and academics do not like marking papers or exams, as they see these as distractions from their primary function, teaching. If the assessment of students' work could be reorganized so as to become part of the main teaching function, rather than separate from it, it might be possible to reduce resistance to and dislike of marking.

- Timely: as well as making work easier, technology should also make it faster. A technological system that ensures that the same task takes longer than it took under the previous system is a waste of resources, unless countervailing value is being added in some other way. Employees will notice this, and will find it frustrating.

- Accountably: finally, as noted above, systems need to enable employees to be held accountable for their work, particularly where issues of trust with outside stakeholders (customers, investors etc.) are involved. Systems should in particular be configured for transparency during operations, rather than *post facto* accountability or scrutiny.

If systems can be created which enables work to be done in these five ways, then it is likely that more employees will see working in virtual space as a natural alternative, and will commit to it. On the other hand, if systems inhibit any one of the five, there is likely to be resistance to virtual working.

Conclusion

Gareth Morgan (1995) argues that, to make virtual organizations work, we need to create new metaphors for understanding them. It is no longer enough to see organizations as machines or biological organisms, or even as some combination of these. New images of organization are needed. We have been living for too long with out-of-date ways of thinking about organizations. Often they use analogies from long-discarded science texts, or writers on organizations rely on second-hand metaphors derived uncritically from other scholars' research.

These new metaphors of organization, whatever they might be, need to take account of human needs and motivations not as side factors which might affect performance, but as issues at the absolute core of how virtual organizations function. For the last decade, economists and organization theorists alike have increasingly been looking at the issue of 'intangible capital', the resources an organization deploys that are seldom if ever listed on a balance sheet but that have an increasingly powerful effect on performance and profitability. The next section of this book looks at intangible capital and how it is used and created in virtual organizations.

Case Study *Royal Air Force Command, 1940*

Following the collapse of France in May and June 1940, Britain was threatened with invasion from Germany. Before a sea-borne invasion could be launched, the German Luftwaffe first needed to defeat the RAF. The German high command believed they had an excellent chance of doing so, as they had a more than 3:1 superiority in numbers of aircraft and pilots. Nonetheless,

▶

within three months the Luftwaffe had been decisively defeated and the German invasion plans postponed indefinitely.

The secret of the RAF's success lay in its development of a simple but highly effective virtual system, based on five elements:

- Radar. Radio-detection finding (RDF) or radar stations detected the approach of German aircraft into British air space. Human operators then passed on details of each contact to RAF Fighter Command headquarters.
- Fighter Command headquarters. Here, the nature and likely target of each German raiding squadron was determined, and orders were passed by telephone to the appropriate sector to deal with the raid.
- Sector commands. These held operational control over the RAF's fighter squadrons. Each sector controller was responsible for allocating squadrons to deal with enemy raiders in his sector. Orders for each squadron were then passed by telephone to the airfield where the squadron was based. Sector command also guided the aircraft to the target once they were airborne.
- Airfields. These were logistics and support units for the squadrons and acted as local managers until the aircraft and pilots were in the air, when control then passed to sector command.
- The fighter squadrons of Spitfires and Hurricanes. When a raid was detected, squadrons were ordered into the air to meet it. Guided by continuous feedback from the radar stations passed along the chain, the fighters were then vectored towards their target. Here the virtual system ended and the conflict became a 'real' one between men and machines.

Though not without its faults, the system was simple and effective, and by the end of the battle squadrons could be in the air on an intercept course as little as 10 minutes after radar first detected the approach of German aircraft. Redundant systems meant that even if one element in the network was knocked out by enemy action, its functions could be easily transferred to another. For example, when an air raid knocked out the sector-command post at Biggin Hill in late August 1940, control of the fighter squadrons based there was simply passed on to the next sector-command post at Kenley. If an airfield was bombed, squadrons could be dispersed to other fields and flown off from there.

The speed and flexibility of the British response allowed the RAF to defeat a much larger enemy. Although technology played a major part, the human factor was the key to the system's success. Technical systems were designed to meet human needs, and the personnel involved, from radar operators to sector controllers to fighter pilots, were thoroughly trained in how to use the system under a variety of contingencies. The system could be seen to be visibly improving the performance of the front-line units, the fighter squadrons, who could get into the air earlier and be more effective when encountering the enemy. And because the RAF had more advance notice of German raids, its commanders could work out creative solutions to counter new German tactics. Lacking a similar system of their own, the German commanders took heavy losses, and the morale of their pilots, who could see no way of defeating the RAF, plummeted. In the end, it was the whole system of radar, telephones, command centres and aircraft, people and machines, that defeated the Luftwaffe and saved Britain from invasion.

Source: Townsend (1971).

Capital in virtual organizations

5 Intangible capital: definitions

At this point, we can sum up what we have said thus far about virtual management and the direction in which we will now proceed. The preceding three chapters have described how virtual organizations are designed and created, how technology systems are used to enable them to function, and the implications this has for work and HRM. Thus far, we have considered virtual organizations primarily from an organizational context in both theoretical and practical terms.

However, there is also an economic aspect to virtual organizations that must be considered when managing them. As virtual organizations are themselves intangible, it might seem logical to conclude that many of their assets are intangible as well. This chapter will deal with this possibility and the ways it may relate to the main theme of this book.

One of the key features of virtual organizations is their strong reliance on intangible capital. The thrust of this chapter defines intangible capital and shows where its economic importance lies. The following chapter looks at how intangible capital is created, used and employed in businesses, and chapter 7 looks at a key part of intangible capital management, the knowledge transformation process. We therefore hope to elucidate the significance of this way of looking at capital.

Once again, much of this section of the book could apply to conventional organizations as well. These too rely on intangible capital to some degree – indeed, no business could do without it. But virtual organizations, by de-emphasizing the physical factors of production, must correspondingly lean more heavily on these intangible factors. The implications of this, in terms of areas such as accounting, valuation of assets, calculation of profitability and return on investment and so on, are considerable. The notion of intangible capital forces us to rethink our approach to business economics, and to apply money – real – values to such intangibles as knowledge, human potential and organizational capabilities.

We will now proceed to trace the intellectual lineage of the concept of intangible capital, and from this, move on to consider its contemporary applicability. In doing so, we can see that the notion is not exactly novel; it antedates the new technology and has been evolving with the modernization process.

Traditional concepts of capital

To eighteenth-century classical economists bound by the conventions of their time, 'capital' was at first a purely physical concept, usually (though not exclusively) in terms of the financial inputs required for production. Other assets such as plant and machinery were also considered under this heading. With some exceptions, the classical approach treated the relationship between the three factors of production – land, labour and capital – as a purely mechanical one. One such exception is Josiah Tucker (1755), an early classical economist who wrote on the problem of human relations in the factory system as it emerged in Britain in his lifetime. Primarily concerned with the prospect of unrest or dispute between the owners of capital and the providers of labour as each tried to maximize their own self-interest, Tucker also touched on the concept that both parties put more into the firm than simply their physical assets or labour. It is to Tucker that we can trace the concept which we here call 'intangible capital' – that is assets with no physical existence and which may not be valuable by conventional methods, but which nonetheless do contribute to and add value to the firm and its operations.

By the time of Adam Smith (on whom Josiah Tucker was a major influence) later in the eighteenth century, this idea was becoming well founded not only in Britain but also in Continental Europe and North America, particularly as Smith's own influence grew (see Schumpeter 1954). As Smith describes it in the opening pages of *The Wealth of Nations* (originally published in 1776), the division of labour is founded in part on the idea that the knowledge and skills required to produce a product can be divided among different employees involved in the production process rather than requiring one employee to master the entire process. Although the division of labour implies that individual employees require less knowledge in order to function (de-skilling), the organization as a whole requires the same level of knowledge as before. Later, in the first chapter of *The Wealth of Nations*, Smith also implicitly recognizes the linkage between knowledge and technology:

> Many improvements have been made by the ingenuity of the makers of the machines, when to make them became the business of a peculiar trade; and some by that of those who are called philosophers or men of speculation, whose trade it is, not to do any thing, but to observe every thing; and who, upon that account, are often capable of combining together the powers of the most distant and dissimilar objects [Smith 1976:21].

Smith implies here, with great insight, that machines function thanks to the knowledge or 'ingenuity' of the people who designed them; machines are in effect outputs of human knowledge, not substitutes for it. He also acknowledges the role of what we now call 'knowledge acquisition' or 'knowledge creation' and notes its role in technology development. This presentation of knowledge as a capital asset was ahead of its time and very innovative. It was more than that: it was seminal, and we can see where its subsequent development by others leads to.

In the nineteenth century, the British classical economist Nassau Senior was more explicit in his description of the role of knowledge. In *Political Economy* (1850), Senior follows the standard view attributed to Smith, that knowledge is a function of labour; he defines labour as 'the voluntary exertion of bodily or mental faculties for the purpose of production' (1850:57), and later says that the productiveness of labour 'depends partly on the corporeal, intellectual and moral qualities of the labourer; on his diligence, his skill, and his strength of body and mind' (1850:175). Here we apparently see the mental qualities of the labourer being put on a par with physical attributes; knowledge (skill) is seen as being as important as physical ability. This view was followed closely by work of the German social thinker and industrialist, Friedrich Engels, exiled in Manchester, who, in discussing how the labour process adds value to the object of labour, states clearly that the labour process question can be either physical or mental. The idea that knowledge adds value to products was by this time clearly established (Engels 1938:65–66). In collaboration with Karl Marx (see Harcourt 2001), they together established a distinct theoretical perspective on this theme, to which we will shortly return.

Senior also offers one of the earliest discussions on the combination of knowledge. The division of knowledge exists to help focus men on particular tasks and increase their specialist skills, he says, but at the same time, those men working on their specialist tasks require co-ordination in order to achieve the end result. This passage (Senior 1850:232–33) hints at the role of general management. It also establishes an interesting point picked up by later writers. The division and recombination of labour are not opposing forces: they are two halves of the same coin. The industrial plants of the Industrial Revolution required two knowledge inputs: on the one hand, the specialist knowledge of workmen, on the other hand, the general knowledge of factory-owners and managers who ensured the process went in the right directions. They are part and parcel of a reciprocal process.

Slightly earlier than Senior, his compatriot Charles Babbage (often credited as the inventor of the computer) had already drawn out the relationship between knowledge and technology in more detail. In his *Economy of Machinery and Manufactures*, a very advanced work for its day, Babbage first discusses the division of labour in fairly conventional, Smithian terms, but then argues (1835:191) that the same principles exactly can be applied to mental labour. The division of labour is not just about managing factories, it is a device 'capable of being employed in preparing the road to some of the sublimest investigations of the human mind'. Babbage appreciated, as few others have before or since, that machines and technology are instruments developed by the human mind, capable of exploring knowledge only with the guiding force of their operators behind them. Machines are tools that greatly magnify human powers, be they physical or mental, but they still require human input at some level, whether in design, operation or both. This recognition of the possibility of labour inputs as not only preconditions for operations but also as leading to 'value-added' is a fascinating insight.

As groundbreaking in terms of intellectual lineage as the above contribution, Karl Marx, in *Das Kapital*, offers a version of labour which focuses yet more directly on the labourer's own abilities, for example: 'labour is a process going on between man and nature, a process in which man, through his own activity, initiates, regulates and controls the material reactions between himself and nature' (1933:169). Starting from where Babbage and Senior left off, Marx argues that it is the labour process that is important. The means of production are just that – means; tools have no function outside the hands of the labourer. The activating forces of the labour process are the physical and especially (we would argue, though Marx does not say so directly) mental energies that the labourer puts into work. More recently, writers on the labour process have extended this notion further (see Braverman 1974; Smith 2001). Such observations became very much *de rigueur* towards the end of the twentieth century in critical writings on work organization, but have tended to attenuate of late.

In 1879, Alfred Marshall, the father of the Cambridge School of economic theory, summed up the debate thus far and noted that: 'As civilisation advances, the relative importance of mental to manual labour changes. Every year mental labour becomes more important and manual labour less important' (1879:9). In other words, mechanization was increasing the dependence on mental labour. The division of labour might be narrowing skills and calling for more specialization, but at the same time it was requiring ever greater levels of skill and knowledge within those specializations. Later, Marshall offers the following views:

> It has already been remarked that the skill and intelligence which are required for commanding and directing the brute forces of nature are growing in importance... Indeed a thorough general education, together with a training for some particular employment, is becoming more necessary to the working man every year. There is scarcely any work which does not need some mental effort [Marshall and Marshall 1879:10–11].

Joseph Schumpeter's theory of the entrepreneur (1934) first developed in Vienna, then later at Harvard, adds another dimension to the subject. He notes the importance of abstract knowledge, but ascribes this more to the role of the inventor/innovator. Entrepreneurship, which he associates with leadership, is dependent as much on psychological qualities and assets as on knowledge in the abstract sense. In other words, the way in which knowledge is used and deployed is as important as the knowledge itself. Talcott Parsons (1959) makes similar comments in his views on the sociology of knowledge elaborated in his Harvard lectures, in which he offers a view of knowledge as a social asset, complementing the earlier views of knowledge as an economic asset. The fact that knowledge is both a social and an economic asset remains of critical importance in understanding how it functions in organizations.

Much the same views have been put forward earlier by the founders of the scientific management movement. The early twentieth-century American scientific management pioneer, Frederick Winslow Taylor, a practitioner contributor to the debate, was often vilified today as the founder of a system that led to de-skilling and the denigration of knowledge. In fact, he was well aware of the importance of knowledge (see Warner 2001). From the beginning, Taylor (1895) argued that the scientific management system could only work if employees were highly skilled and educated. Taylor believed that both background general knowledge and task-specific knowledge was required, and that both had an influence on how well employees would perform their function. He went further: firms which adopted scientific management, he said, would attract the most skilled and knowledgeable workers, as these would recognize that such firms could better reward them for the use and application of their skills and knowledge. As Drucker (1999:81) later put it, 'Taylor was the first person to apply knowledge to work'. He showed that it was knowledge that made people productive not manual work *per se*, perhaps implicitly criticizing Marx's view that labour was, in itself, the source of value. Work has to be planned, organized and executed; here it is knowledge that shapes the management process that utilizes labour to create wealth.

Taylor's views were echoed by other writers on scientific management; these included most notably his compatriot Harrington Emerson (1913). Later, the management functions were divided into 'line' and 'staff' by writers such as Lyndall Urwick (1933), a management consultant in Britain who also explicitly recognizes the role of organizational knowledge, which is categorized into specialist (for line functions) and general or overall (for staff functions) (see Brech 2002). Staff management, in this conception, is largely a knowledge management function. Further twentieth-century writers on management, most notably Drucker (1999) in North America, have continued to stress the importance of knowledge, particularly for general management (Warner and Witzel 1998).

In the late twentieth century, these ideas coalesced in the idea of 'intangible capital'. Three aspects of intangible capital have been commonly defined: human capital, organizational capital and knowledge capital.

Intangible capital: types and sources

Human capital

Human beings are, according to conventional wisdom, tangible and in their tangible form they provide the production input known as labour. But the workings of the human brain are not tangible, and it is in the brain's knowledge capabilities and thought processes that intangible human capital resides. Daly (2001), for example, has described human capital as the investment a firm makes in developing the potential of its people. Development nearly always takes place on a mental plane, 'inside' the brain; in other words, investing in human capital means increasing the collective brainpower of the organization. Davis and Meyer (1998) choose to define human capital as the relationships people have with others, valuing them for their connections as much as for themselves. Both these definitions are undoubtedly important. New technology has expanded the degree of intangibility.

Human capital and knowledge capital are inextricably bound together. Just as knowledge needs an active agency to achieve utility, so the human brain without knowledge is an empty vessel, capable only of carrying out basic instinctive and functional tasks. It can be argued that the human mind is not the only agency capable of exploiting knowledge capital – computer applications are able to do the same thing in cyberspace – but it is important to remember that the human mind and the computer function in quite different ways, as has been pointed out by Oxford neurobiologist Susan Greenfield (1997) among others. Human capital derives value not only from what knowledge it possesses, but also from how it acts upon that knowledge. The capacities of the human mind for emotion and intuition are both the greatest advantage of human capital and the greatest barrier to its effective management.

Organizational capital

Another way of looking at the same problem is in terms of what we may call organizational capital.

Tremblay (1995) has defined organizational capital as 'embodied in the persons composing the organization (rather than its technology or machines) and cannot be appropriated in any individual'. Organizational capital, then, is organization-specific and inclusive; ideally, it should reflect the sum of all knowledge and human capital within the organization, as well as all organizational systems that encourage and facilitate the use of both. According to Davis and Meyer (1998), organizational capital (which they call structural capital) consists of 'all the firm-standard business processes, systems, and policies that represent the accumulation of experience and learning by many people over many years'. Warner and Witzel (1998) have previously equated organizational capital with general management; it is the task of the general manager to encourage the acquisition, creation, use and diffusion of knowledge within the firm. One of the general manager's core tasks is thus the management of organizational capital.

Knowledge capital

One of the earliest thinkers to conceptualize knowledge in terms we may recognize today was Plato. On its own, 'knowledge' is a static concept; it can be stored, in books, on electronic media or in human minds, but it needs an activating force. Much more recently, Drucker (1989:242) has defined knowledge as 'information that changes something or somebody – either by becoming grounds for action, or by making an individual (or an institution) capable of different and more effective action'. Definitions of knowledge capital also take it to mean knowledge that is available to a firm and which can be actively employed for the purposes suggested by Drucker. Most definitions treat knowledge as having an asset value. Witzel (2000), for instance, defines knowledge capital loosely as the asset value inherent in any organization or person that is derived directly from the knowledge possessed by them. Davis and Meyer (1998:202) regard knowledge capital as 'knowledge for sale'. In practical terms, this often means things such as patents or copyrights, which represent accumulated knowledge and have market value. Properly, though, knowledge capital should include any asset that derives its value in part or whole from accumulated knowledge, whether that knowledge has been generated within the company or acquired from outside sources.

The relationship between these three forms of intangible capital and the role of the general manager is suggested in figure 5.1. Organizational capital is here seen as the intangible framework of the organization, setting the parameters of its knowledge and guiding the processes of knowledge transformation (described in more detail below). Human capital consists of the individual functioning elements within the firm that in turn serve to interpret and exploit knowledge capital; the latter can either be acquired from outside the firm or generated within it (again described below).

The role of intangible capital in conventional organizations

How these three elements of intangible capital are interrelated is described by Japanese organization theorists, Nonaka and Takeuchi (1995:59):

> In a strict sense, knowledge is created only by individuals. An organization cannot create knowledge without individuals. The organization supports creative individuals or provides contexts for them to create knowledge. Organizational knowledge creation, therefore, should be understood as a process that 'organizationally' amplifies the knowledge created by individuals and crystallizes it as part of the knowledge network of the organization.

These thinkers also make explicit the link between knowledge and belief or commitment. Thus, if we conceive of organizational capital acting as a kind of enabling framework, human capital provides the agency which creates and exploits knowledge. This framework closely matches the concept of virtual space set out in chapters 2–4.

Just as with the physical factors of production, so intangible capital enables firms to add value. It does so in five ways. It might help to conceive of these five ways as a nexus of forces, similar to the 'five forces' model developed by Michael Porter (1980) at the Harvard Business School. Porter's model defines the forces that influence a marketplace; our model, shown in figure 5.3, shows the forces that influence the nature and extent of an organization's virtual capital and its ability to add value. Four of the five forces – skills, innovation, knowledge of the market and knowledge of the environment – are independent variables; how they are managed, their nature and size is determined by the fifth force, internal co-ordination.

- Innovation adds value through new products and services and improvements to existing ones, including the whole bundle of benefits such as better service delivery etc. Innovation can also make improvements to production and delivery processes, yielding better quality and/or cost savings.

Figure 5.1 Relationship between forms of intangible capital

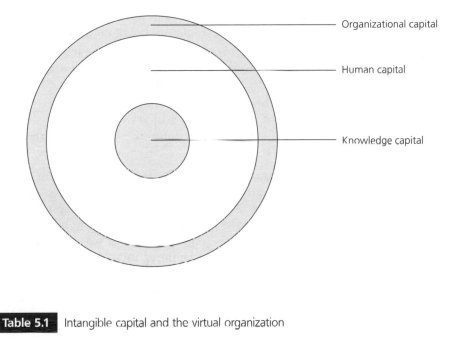

Organizational capital

Human capital

Knowledge capital

Table 5.1 Intangible capital and the virtual organization

	Intangible capital	*Virtual organization*
Space	Knowledge capital	Knowledge
Enabling mechanism	Organizational capital	Technology
Agency	Human capital	Human resources

Figure 5.2 The five forces of intangible capital

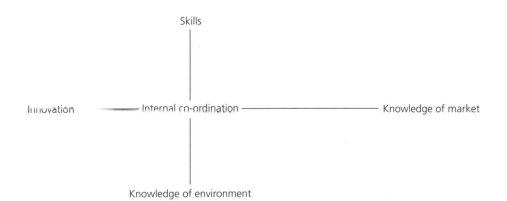

Skills

Innovation ——— Internal co-ordination ——————— Knowledge of market

Knowledge of environment

- Skills add value through improved quality of design and production, meaning better, more reliable and cheaper products and services.
- Knowledge of the market enables the company to tailor its offerings to market needs, to find niches whose needs are not being met, and so on.
- Knowledge of the environment enables the company to note moves made by competitors, changes in the economic and regulatory environment and so on, and to adapt and adjust to these in a timely manner.
- Internal co-ordination makes the company run more efficiently and effectively, with cost savings and other value-added that may be passed on to customers. Internal co-ordination also determines how effectively the other five factors are being used.

Intangible capital, then, is not just a matter of gathering and storing knowledge. Knowledge only adds value when it is put into action through human agency, in one of the five ways shown above. Many theories of intangible capital regard its possession as a virtue in its own right; an organization's intangible capital is measured by how much knowledge it has acquired; in other words, how much the organization knows. We argue that the value of intangible capital is the value it can add through its employment in one of these five forces. In other words, intangible capital is only of value if it can contribute – even indirectly – to the bottom line.

Intangible capital and virtual space

Once again, these five aspects of virtual capital have implications for all business organizations, not just virtual ones. However, they are of particular importance for virtual organizations. Because they rely less on physical factors of production, especially land, and locate more of their operations in knowledge-dependent virtual space, virtual organizations are heavily dependent on the five forces of intangible capital. For example:

- Innovation in virtual space. Innovation is especially important in virtual space for two, complementary reasons. First, of course, one of the reasons for moving into virtual space is to meet customer needs more effectively, whether through a combination of new, virtually delivered products, a more efficient and effective business system, or both. In all these cases, innovation either in products or processes is a prerequisite. Because most of the technologies that create virtual space are easy to obtain, there is little technological lead time over competitors, and it is only by constant innovation that firms can stay ahead. Second, neither the implementation of virtual technology nor the subsequent innovation processes are cost free, and the manager has to be sure that innovations will add real value.
- Skills in virtual space. Because people in virtual organizations work remotely on their own or in small groups, the level of division of labour is much lower; workers and managers require a much greater depth and breadth of

skills than workers and managers in large concentrated organizations. Further, while working in virtual space continues to require all the old management skills, it also requires some new ones. How do we manage quality virtually? How do we account for our work and our assets virtually? How do we learn and create knowledge in virtual space? These and other issues need to be addressed by the virtual manager.

- Knowledge of the market in virtual space. In chapter 2, we suggested that firms marketing to their customers through virtual space face a disadvantage compared to traditional retailers where customers walk through the door and are seen face to face. The virtual marketer has to 'imagine' his or her customers on the basis of the data and feedback available. There is therefore a much higher premium on initiating customer contact: if the virtual marketer wants to know something about a customer or group of customers, it is likely that he or she will have to go to the customers and ask them, rather than waiting for a customer to come along. Managing this kind of two-way proactive customer contact requires new skills and new ways of handling knowledge.

- Knowledge of the environment in virtual space. Here the change from conventional organizations to virtual organizations is more one of degree than of kind. Management in virtual space tends to be more fluid, and the speed and incidence of change are much higher. The steady introduction of new forms of technology is in part responsible for this (as witness the current development of broadband, threatening Internet technology with obsolescence barely a decade after its development). Governments are still grappling with how to regulate virtual space, and new and unexpected initiatives can arise here as well. For these and other reasons, knowledge of the environment and the ability to react quickly to environmental change are vitally important in virtual space.

- Internal co-ordination in virtual space. This is the same old problem of co-ordinating the organization's activities, but cast in a new light. 'Explicitly recognizing knowledge as a corporate asset is new, as is understanding the need to manage and invest it with the same care paid to getting value from other, more tangible assets' (Davenport 1998). The problems of co-ordination are magnified by time and distance, and careful design of technological systems (see chapter 3) is required to ensure that these barriers are reduced as far as possible, while at the same time the firm's human elements need to be motivated and kept focused on the organization's goals (see chapter 4). Co-ordination can take up even more of a manager's time when working in virtual space than in conventional organizations, because of the constant need not only to keep in touch with subordinates, but also to make sure they are keeping in touch with each other.

Conclusion

Earlier in this book we described knowledge as the lifeblood of the organization. There are other metaphors, for example Edvinsson's (1997) description of intellectual capital (knowledge) as the heartwood of the organizational tree. In this chapter we have sought to show that the concept of intangible capital in its various forms is not new; what is new is our belated recognition of its importance and value. We have shown how intangible capital is employed in organizations, and noted its increased importance for the highly knowledge-dependent virtual organizations. In the next chapter, we seek to show how intangible capital is created, costed and valued. The following chapter, chapter 7, then looks at how knowledge is actually used in order to create value in its own right.

Case Study *The World Bank*

The World Bank has been in operation for over fifty years, and not without controversy. It has one of the largest stores of knowledge capital in the world, most of which is human-based (that is based on the skills and personal knowledge of the bank's staff) and is focused on the bank's goal of reducing global poverty through capital lending and knowledge-sharing. The focus on knowledge-sharing is relatively new, however; prior to 1996, the organization's core focus was on development lending. However, attempts to achieve its goal as a lending organization generally failed, as there was little agreement on the nature of the relationship between reducing poverty and capital funding, even though the latter sometimes reached US$30 billion a year. In 1996 the focus began to change, thanks to the following incident.

In June 1995, a health worker in a small town in Zambia, one of the poorest countries in the world, logged onto the website for the centre for disease control in Atlanta, Georgia. The worker was able to get an answer to a question on how to treat malaria. The most important part of the story for the World Bank is that the bank wasn't involved at all. It became obvious that the bank did not have its knowledge organized in such a way that it was available to the people who make decisions about development around the world.

Through this example and others like it, the bank realized that, while the mission of the organization was to reduce poverty, there were several means to achieving this goal. Lending was one such means, but sharing knowledge was another. This led to a vision of a different kind of organization. An internal movement began within the bank, championing the concept of the World Bank as a 'knowledge bank'.

In October 1996, with the endorsement of its president, the World Bank decided to put together a small group of people to facilitate the new mission, called the KM Group. The group, comprising a handful of people, led the

▶

transformation of the organization into a knowledge bank. Their mandate was to develop and implement a knowledge-sharing budget, to build a new personnel model that included over 100 communities of practice, to align the technology that would be necessary to facilitate knowledge-sharing, and then to monitor the results. From the perspective of Stephen Denning, then Director of the KM Group, one of the primary roles of the bank was to help countries to capitalize on the new knowledge economy by promoting:

- an economic and institutional framework, to provide incentives for the efficient use of existing knowledge, the creation of new knowledge and the flourishing of entrepreneurship;
- an educated and skilled population, which could create, share and use knowledge;
- a dynamic information infrastructure, to facilitate the effective communication, dissemination and processing of information and knowledge;
- a network of knowledge centres, including research centres, universities, think tanks and community groups, to tap into the growing stock of global knowledge, assimilate and adapt it to local needs and create new knowledge.

With this in mind, the KM Group set out to make the bank a clearing-house for knowledge about development, a 'corporate memory' of best practices, and a collector and disseminator of the best development knowledge from around the world.

Knowledge management at the bank is carried out through eight principal activities:

- building communities of practice (of which the core members are called 'thematic groups');
- developing an online knowledge base in which bank know-how is stored and from which it can be made widely accessible;
- establishing help desks and advisory services;
- building a directory of expertise;
- making available key sectoral statistics;
- providing access to transaction or engagement information;
- providing a dialogue space for professional conversations;
- establishing external access and outreach to external clients, partners and stakeholders.

The knowledge management strategy at the bank is enabled by its IT technology infrastructure, which is accessible by everyone. The main focus here is on making knowledge widely accessible through the World Wide Web.

The Bank has also launched several new global knowledge initiatives in partnership with the private sector, international and bilateral agencies, non-governmental organizations and others to tackle key social, financial and technological challenges. These new partnerships lie at the heart of the bank's vision of knowledge for all. Denning sums up the future role of knowledge management in economic development:

A different kind of conception of development will emerge in which knowledge is not only on the par with money; knowledge becomes the driver. One could imagine a world in which communities of practice, and networks of communities of practice became the theme and money became the support to these communities of practice in a highly decentralised fashion. That would be quite a different vision of development from the last fifty years that has essentially been around money – the process of transferring money from one group to another group and hoping that some development would occur as part of it. A different vision is now emerging in which development would be a process of sharing knowledge, and putting better proposals in place, which would then be supported by money. The main emphasis would be on getting top-quality knowledge to focus on the problems.

Source: Ramona Dzinkowski, 'Knowledge for All: Knowledge Sharing at the World Bank', *Mastering Management Online*, July 2002.

6 Intangible capital: sources and value

The previous chapter showed how the concept of intangible capital, in economic terms, has actually been around for a long time. Only very recently, however, has the idea entered management theory, and only within the last decade and a half have people begun to work on practical methods for deploying and using intangible capital.

Because intangible capital is intangible, managing it poses a special set of problems. The first issue to be resolved is, where does intangible capital come from? How is it generated or acquired? Second, intangible capital is not, in most cases, a free good; there are costs associated with its acquisition and maintenance. What are these and how can they be measured? Third, and perhaps most problematic, what is the value of intangible capital? How can its value be defined, and how can its returns be measured? A number of authors (most recently Lev 2002) have commented on this problem; it appears that traditional book-keeping and accounting systems are unable to account for intangible capital, and that new methods of accounting are necessary if intangible capital is to be valued and accounted for in terms of its real worth.

This is not an abtruse accounting issue: it has very serious implications for how organizations reliant on intangible capital raise funds. Menendez-Olonso (2002) has noted a relationship between financial capital structure and intangible assets: firms with high levels of intangible capital tend, for example, to have lower debt levels. This is not deliberate; instead, these firms have more difficulty in raising capital through the debt markets. Since the dotcom crash, they are having more difficulty in raising money through the capital markets as well. This is rapidly becoming a critical issue for many businesses, not just those that are structured as virtual organizations.

Virtual organizations, by their nature, are heavily dependent on intangible capital, and therefore these issues are of first-water importance for managers in virtual organizations. In the previous chapter we quoted Davenport (1998) to the effect that companies needed to learn how to use and invest intangible capital in exactly the same way as conventional, tangible forms of capital. It is important to note here that intangible capital complements conventional capital. Other factor inputs – land and, to a lesser extent, labour (though as chapters 4 and 5 both suggest, the importance of the human element is greatly magnified when dealing with intangible capital) – can be substituted or reduced. Intangible capital and tangible capital are codependent. The five value-adding activities connected with intangible capital discussed in the previous chapter all require investment in terms of both finance and other assets.

As we noted in chapter 1, the dotcom companies that failed were not usually undercapitalized – many had at least as much money as they needed – but they were badly capitalized in the sense that there was no fit between tangible and intangible capital. The money invested did not go to back up the knowledge and organizational assets that the dotcom companies possessed, but was spent on business activities that would never have more than a marginal impact. The example of fashion retailer Boo.com shows clearly how tangible capital was invested in style rather than substance, and intangible capital, starved of support, was unable to be effective and add value.

The issues discussed above are important and complex ones, and there is not time to deal with them here. A number of sources (Davenport 1998; Svelby 1997; Edvinsson 1997; Stewart 1997; Menendez-Olonso 2002; Lev 2002) discuss them in more detail. What we are most concerned with here is the relationship between intangible capital and virtual organizations, and we will consider briefly the main problems of acquiring and valuing intangible capital in that light.

Sources of intangible capital

Intangible capital may come in a number of forms. First, there is what we might call 'conventional' intangible capital. The oldest and most widely recognized form of intangible capital that businesses own is goodwill, the existence of which is now universally recognized. Accountants and tax inspectors may quibble about the valuation on this form of capital, but its existence is not particularly problematic. Another long-recognized form comes under the general heading of 'intellectual capital', usually referring to holdings such as copyrights, patents, trademarks and so on. Again, the exact valuation of these can be questionable, but they can be seen to be assets thanks to their potential to generate income and/or partially protect the company's products and services from competitors. Intangible property is often represented as 'intellectual property right' (O'Hara and Peak 2000:119). Hardware is tangible but software is not, and so is seen as intangible. Whether it is capital *de facto* depends on its valuation; it may however have a potential value. A more recent addition to the stable is brand equity. By the early 1990s, it had become widely recognized that a company's portfolio of brands, and the value-added these represented, were an asset in their own right and should be accounted for.

All of the above are forms of organizational capital. In knowledge terms, it is tempting to classify these as outputs that are created by the company's operations. Goodwill grows out of relationships cultivated with customers, suppliers etc.; intellectual property derives from the efforts of R&D and design departments; brand equity is a by-product of the company's marketing efforts and so on (of course these can be reinvested in the company and become factor inputs in turn).

Much more difficult to recognize and value are input forms of intangible capital such as knowledge capital and human capital, referred to in the previous chapter, along with other forms of organizational capital such as business systems and processes, firm policies and strategies, organizational culture and so on. Every organization has these, but there is no consensus on how they should be recognized or on where they come from. No corporation refers to these in their balance sheet; at best, they merit a few paragraphs in the annual report. Yet they are critical to business success: virtual organizations in particular cannot survive without them.

In effect, there are three sources or generators of intangible capital inputs: people, technology and organizations. Below, we discuss each of these and their relationship with the three forms of intangible capital.

People as creators

People are one of the best sources of intangible capital, and paradoxically this is even more true of technologically sophisticated firms. Recognition of the importance of people in this respect goes back to the classical economists of the eighteenth century; for example, Adam Smith compared 'educating' a trained worker to spending money on an expensive machine (Smith 1776:118). Both would bring returns on the capital invested.

People make contributions to each of the three classes of intangible capital. First and foremost there is their own personal stock of pre-existing knowledge, their skills and capabilities, and particularly their intellectual abilities, including not only basic IQ but also reasoning and analytical abilities and so on. These latter are often more important than basic intelligence, and the ability to learn is of greater value than existing knowledge (important though the latter may be). Through their own brainpower and ability to analyse, reason and create, people make contributions individually to a firm's stock of knowledge capital.

However, this knowledge has to be shared or disseminated in some way. The best knowledge management organizations are those that enable members of the

Table 6.1 Sources and types of intangible capital

Types	People	Technology	Organization
Knowledge capital	Brainpower; personal human creativity	Analytical and modelling tools etc.	Organizational forms and cultures that facilitate knowledge management
Human capital	Sharing creative experience and knowledge	Technology that enhances personal effort	HRM and 'investment in people'
Organizational capital	Team-working and taskforces for research and innovation	Communications networks and others that facilitate efficiency and effectiveness	Strategies and structures

organization to learn from each other and to create synergies that will generate new knowledge. The development and dissemination of new knowledge in this fashion improves the ability of workers and managers, singly and collectively, to perform their various tasks and functions. This increases the firm's stock of human capital. This idea is one of the underpinning concepts of the learning organization (Senge 1990).

Finally, people work together in taskforces or teams to create and generate knowledge internally and to acquire it from outside sources. The development of team-working practices in this way adds also to the firm's organizational capital, creating a culture where flexibility, creativity and innovation are accepted norms.

Technology as creator

We have been keen to stress throughout this book so far that technology is a series of artefacts, inert and value neutral without human operators to drive it. Nevertheless, technology can be a source of intangible capital depending on how it is used and structured. It is important to remember that this does not refer only to information and communications technologies, but to all forms of technology used by the firm: in fact, as Zeleny (2000:xv) has commented, 'All technology is becoming information technology (IT)'.

An example of a type of technology that is frequently used to help create intangible capital is software, itself a highly intangible asset: apart from disks and instruction manuals, software exists as a series of coded signals in virtual space. At the knowledge capital level, for example, analytical and modelling tools help humans to search data, refine their results and generate higher levels of information and knowledge. In human capital terms, developing skills and experience at using various software tools enhances the capabilities of a firm's people. Finally, communications networks and other software tools can be used to enhance the firm's organizational structure and make it more efficient and effective; in particular, as noted previously, they enable virtual organizational forms to exist.

It is important to note, though, that technology on its own does not contribute to intangible capital. How we turn technology into business value is through 'knowledge of usage', not 'mere fact of possession' (Zeleny 2000:xv). Technology as a creator of intangible capital requires human agency as well.

Organizations as creators

The organization's strategy, structure and culture frequently has an important impact on the generation of intangible capital at all levels. At the level of knowledge management, the organization can structure itself in such a way as to manage knowledge more effectively, thus adding value to individual and team knowledge-creation efforts. At the level of human capital, the organization can choose to deliberately invest in developing human potential through the HRM department and through other channels. Finally, at the level of organizational capital, organizational strategy, structure, goal-setting and leadership themselves contribute to the organization's ability to deliver to customers and to succeed competitively. Organizational capital is thus partly a self-generating process: good organizations tend to evolve organically into better organizations.

Just as technology requires human agency to function, so organizations require both human agency and technology to generate intangible capital. Organizations exist as a mix of human and mechanical functions, and it is the fit between these functions and the synergy they generate that creates additional capital over and above their own efforts.

Costs of intangible capital

Intangible capital, however, is not a free good. Its development and maintenance carry associated costs. Technology maintenance, HRM investments, training and so on all represent costs of intangible capital. Costing these intangibles, and calculating the cost–return ratio, is a key challenge for the manger of the virtual organization.

People costs

People costs arise from not only recruitment and selection of high-value employees, but also their training and development. It is generally agreed that training and development are continuous, career-long processes, and there will always be costs associated with these: fees to trainers, opportunity costs generated by the time employees take off work to undergo training, costs of covering for the absentees while they are being trained and so on. All these intangible costs can be described as 'people maintenance' and usually come out of the HRM department's budget.

So expensive are skilled employees to recruit and maintain that firms are sometimes tempted to cut corners in this area, particularly with regard to training. Yet from an intangible capital perspective, this is very dangerous. People cannot contribute effectively to a firm's overall human capital and organizational capital unless they have the knowledge and the skills to do so. People who are not engaged in training or development are not increasing their personal stock of knowledge/skills, and risk being left behind by those continuing to advance. As with people, so it is with firms. In the end, one powerful reason for engaging in training may be that your competitors are doing so.

But there are also private, organizational and social returns from investing in people (Daly 2001). It is not only the quantity (number) of personnel selected but also their quality that is critical. Getting the human mix right within the organization creates a valuable asset; getting the mix wrong can be disastrous.

Technology costs

Technology maintenance is a primary intangible cost. We are talking here primarily about software, as opposed to investment in hardware or its replacement. Software and network maintenance and management are huge ongoing costs, as well as the upgrading and the adaptation of systems. *The Economist* (21 September 2002) noted that the numbers of IT people needed to support the increasing complexity of systems and the billion individuals and the millions of firms involved on the Internet may soon be over 200 million, or about two-thirds of the population of the US.

The costs of technology in this respect should come down. For example, Sun Microsystems has recently unveiled N1, its new 'virtualization' tool that aims to cut out vast layers of system administrators. The costs of selecting, recruiting and maintaining technological resources, and the human operatives they require, could be correspondingly reduced. But technology costs will never be entirely eliminated, and will continue to form an element of overheads.

Value provided by intangible capital

In exchange for these costs, intangible capital in turn provides value to the firm that develops, acquires and owns it. It does so in two ways; by adding value to existing products and services, and by generating potential future value for customers (and thus for shareholders).

Added value can be created through the application of intangible capital at any point along the value chain. The following are just a small proportion of the ways in which this can be done:

- Sourcing: knowledge capital can lead to more effective sourcing of higher quality and/or cheaper raw materials and components. Human capital can lead to the sourcing process itself becoming more efficient and effective, reducing other factor costs. Organizational capital can link the sourcing process with design and production functions, reducing internal transaction costs.

- R&D/design: knowledge capital plays a pivotal role in creation and innovation, particularly in ensuring that product features meet customer needs. Human capital helps bring together the research and design teams needed to take initial innovations forward and develop them further. Organizational capital transforms research and design concepts into marketable products.

- Production: knowledge capital helps to design production systems for maximum efficiency and effectiveness. Human capital ensures the application of the relevant skills and the right composition of the production team. Organizational capital links production to other departments and ensures feedback is channelled forwards and backwards to improve production.

- Quality management: knowledge capital determines what quality is and what the standards should be. Human capital provides the understanding of how to achieve quality and how standards should be employed. Organizational capital makes certain that quality is everyone's business, and promotes cultures such as continuous improvement and total-quality management.

- Distribution: knowledge capital understands consumer needs and develops the best and most effective distribution system. Human capital ensures the system functions smoothly and efficiently with the least level of stock losses or shortages. Organizational capital ties the distribution system to production and marketing and ensures a smooth flow of products and services to consumers.

- Marketing: knowledge capital understands consumer needs and develops solutions to those needs. Human capital goes on to provide the link between customer and the organization; understanding and even empathizing with customer needs is an important human quality. Organizational capital is then invested in the marketing effort through the deployment of human and knowledge resources to generate brands and brand equity.

- Post-marketing: knowledge capital continues to research customer needs and determine whether goods and services are providing satisfaction. Human capital again provides the necessary understanding and empathy with the consumer. Organizational capital ensures that any loss of customer satisfaction is taken seriously and meets with an immediate response from other parts of the organization.

- Organization: behind the scenes, in the back office and at top-management level, knowledge capital generates strategies, goals and targets for the organization as a whole. Human capital provides skills, vision and leadership to enable goals to be met. Organizational capital provides a structure and framework within which the whole functions at the best possible level. As noted above, organizational capital is in part a self-reproducing form of capital; good organizations tend, in an organic fashion, to become better.

Future value is a more problematic form of value created by intangible capital, as it consists of potential rather present value. We have earlier defined knowledge as 'the stored potential for action'. The corollary of this is that not all of an organization's knowledge capital will be in use at any one time; some of it, at least, will be stored and ready for future use, but will not have immediate applicability.

Knowledge currently in use is making a contribution to the bottom line. Knowledge stored for future use obviously has a potential to influence the bottom line in future, but it is impossible to know exactly in what way and to what extent. Knowing how much knowledge to acquire and store is an interesting problem for companies. If too little knowledge capital is available, then innovation and creativity may be hampered; going to the opposite extreme may mean devoting excessive effort to knowledge management activities and, in turn, taking effort away from other equally vital activities. (A corollary would be buying extra land, or taking on extra staff, to enable growth and expansion: the additional assets have to be commensurate with the expected growth.) These sorts of value issues need to be considered with managing knowledge capital.

Similarly, human capital has a future value as well as a present value. Every employee will make a contribution to productivity and profitability over the course of the time that he or she remains with the company. But how long will the employee remain? Also, the longer an employee remains with the company, the greater his or her human capital contribution should become: he or she will be better trained, have more skills, develop more experience, create more knowledge and probably be promoted into a position of greater responsibility. But at what rate, and to what levels, can the contribution be expected to rise? These are important issues for valuing human capital, and should be addressed by the HRM department at the very least.

Finally, there is future organizational capital. We have mentioned that good organizations become, in an organic sense, better organizations: continuous improvement means that structures, systems, leadership etc. become of better quality. Strategies are refined down and become more realistic. But how do you value a strategy, or a management system? What value is attached to leadership? These decisions, when made at all, tend to be made in a very *ad hoc* way. Since the collapse of the dotcom bubble, venture capitalists and lenders have begun concentrating more on the potential of the management team of companies in which they are investing, and clearly see management as a value-creating activity both for the present and for the future. But valuation of such ability is at best a subjective measure.

Measuring the value of intangible capital

As noted, a number of authors have commented on the weakness of traditional systems of accounting when it comes to intangible capital. Warner and Witzel (2000) believe that this is an issue which requires urgent attention, and Lev (2002:1) has called for:

> a stock taking of the accumulated knowledge about intangible (intellectual) assets with particular emphasis on the economic laws governing intangibles, the lessons to be drawn from the extensive research on intangibles, the private and social harms related to information deficiencies concerning intangibles, and ways to overcome these deficiencies.

Cummins (2002) notes that so far no direct measures have evolved for measuring the value of intangible capital, and that therefore indirect measures are used instead. He cites two methods:

● The stock-market approach: to take the corporation's equity value and subtract from it the value of its tangible assets. What remains must be intangible assets. As Cummins notes, this method is susceptible to many fluxes and there is no guaranteeing that the stock-market valuation will be an accurate reflection of the corporation's real value, as the example of Enron showed all too clearly.

- The analysts' forecast approach: similar to the above, but instead, analysts' expected forecasts of firm value are used as the benchmark; again, the value of tangible assets is subtracted, and the remainder is considered to be the value of the intangible assets. This has the advantage of being some-what more realistic than the stock-market approach (though analysts too can be wrong), and also allows for a calculation of future value as well as present value-added.

Cummins adopts the second method, and concludes that while the traditional output types of intangible capital such as intellectual property, noted above, often have a marginal product that is somewhat less than their marginal cost. Input-type organizational capital, on the other hand, is very valuable, with a marginal product of about 70 per cent annually (Cummins 2002:27). It should be added that this way of calculating intangible capital needs to be verified, and there are flaws in the logic of Cummins's approach: he argues that, because intangible capital cannot be replicated between firms (the value of an employee or a computer system lies in how it is used, not in the person or system itself; recall Strassman's [1990] argument that a computer on its own is worth no more than its value at auction), intangible capital is not an input *per se*, but a way of combining traditional factor inputs such as land, labour and capital. This approach ignores the role of knowledge as a factor input, calling the method into question.

Cummins shows that it is possible to begin thinking about the idea of valuing intangible assets. The major flaw in such approaches, though, is that they value only the whole of a company's intangible assets, and not the value of individual assets. And any attempt to reach a value in this way is dependent on the highly subjective valuation of the company as a whole.

When valuing intangible assets, a degree of subjectivity is inevitable. Why not, therefore, introduce that subjectivity at a lower level, and make subjective judgements about the value of each intangible asset or class of assets? A total valuation based on a series of subjective judgements is no more likely to be wrong that one based on a single subjective judgement, and in the process of examining assets and making these judgements the firm is likely to learn more about its own intangible capital and how it is used, knowledge that will not come from staring at a lump sum on a balance sheet.

As described above, intangible capital has two kinds of value: added value and future value. Calculations of current added value should be possible in the same way that a firm measures added value more generally. The difference between the value of the factor inputs and the value of the total output is the value-added by the firm: managers then need to ask what portion of that addi-tional value derives from intangible capital. The answer is likely to be a large portion, although the exact amount will differ given the nature of the firm, the nature of its products and services, firm structure etc.

Some forms of intangible capital are now frequently measured. Brand equity, a concept barely heard of a decade ago, is one example; Keller (1997) devotes three chapters of a book on strategic brand management to the measurement of brand equity. Srinivasan (2002) develops what he calls the 'equity map' approach, in which various contributing factors to brand equity are measured and their impact on overall brand equity can be monitored. It is possible that techniques of this kind can serve as models for developing measures of other forms of intangible capital.

The case of future value is more problematic. The key problems are of verification and predictability. A firm may state that it has stocks of knowledge capital to a certain value, but who is to verify this, given the subjective nature of much knowledge itself? And how can future value be predicted? There are two possible approaches here. One is to take the total measure of intellectual capital described by Cummins, projected forward and then broken down into various value streams, with a notional value assigned to each. The other, more difficult but probably more rewarding, is to identify individual value streams – the level of skills or of education of employees, management performance, organizational culture etc. – and try to assess their ongoing value potential.

Part of the problem of measuring value from intangible capital, of course, is that initial returns expected from it in the 1990s did not always materialize. There has even developed a certain scepticism about the whole concept, and given recent events this is understandable. The year 1999 and early 2000 saw the share price of Internet companies go for a 'rollercoaster ride', shooting up and then down again as the market tried to figure out what, if anything, these companies were actually worth. Eventually it decided most of them were worth nothing, and the market crashed.

The dotcom economy created a bubble, true; but how realistic was the judgement that most of these companies were valueless? In the end, lacking any other substantive measures – such as profits – the market decided not to place any value on their intangible assets; as most of them had few tangible assets, their value fell to the floor. It can be argued that the share price of a virtual company (not all Internet stocks were virtual companies, but the two have enough common features to be comparable here) is a reflection of the value of the knowledge that company has – in other words, its knowledge capital. But how does an investor make a return if that knowledge cannot be turned into profit? Many Internet companies have never made a profit; even now, some of the survivors never will. Knowledge is static; investing in knowledge alone is like investing in a pile of rocks. Human capital is required to make that knowledge active and at least potentially profitable.

Internet companies are not alone in this regard, and many other examples can be found, including consultancy firms and biotech companies. As knowledge-based, virtual companies and sectors multiply, the problem will become more pressing. There is an urgent need for an accurate and effective means of valuing all three kinds of intangible asset: knowledge capital, human capital and organizational capital. What is knowledge worth on its own? What is the value of a skilled and creative employee? What is the bottom-line impact of accumulated organizational capital? What would the loss of an intangible asset mean in terms of profitability?

These are not the kinds of value that fit easily – or at all – into balance sheets and annual financial statements. They are subjective, and subject to fluctuation as times change. But they do represent real and potential value. Some form of quantification of these is necessary, if only to secure continued investment. As Menendez-Olonso (2002) points out, companies that rely heavily on intangible capital have trouble securing investment because investors do not know how to value their assets. We cannot pretend that we have the solutions to this problem here and now, but we argue that solutions will have to be found in the very near future. If we are going to truly make progress towards a knowledge economy, this hurdle has to be cleared. The onus is on everyone – companies, auditors, analysts and regulators – to work together to develop reliable and satisfactory measures for valuing intangible capital.

Conclusion

Where, then, does this leave our virtual manager? Ultimately, it is not enough to have intangible capital; it must either be used in a value-adding way or be shown to have the potential for value in the future. In the course of managing intangible capital, managers need to consider it as capital in exactly the same way that they would tangible assets.

For the manager in a virtual organization, this issue becomes still more pressing. Tangible assets are fewer, and may not even be central to the company's operations, needs or performance. If the company relies on the valuation of its assets to raise capital in debt or equity markets, for example, then this can present real problems, especially in today's sceptical climate.

We noted above that there is a pressing need to develop a reliable and generally accepted way of accounting for intangible assets. However, we doubt that such a method will be developed until such time as the managers of intangible capital-dependent organizations – especially virtual organizations – learn how to concentrate on the core-value issues and how to leverage intangible capital in order to create current and future value-added. To do this, they need to learn to manage intangible capital more effectively, and it is here that the crux of the issue lies.

The following chapter discusses one of the fundamental issues behind intangible capital, the management of knowledge. We present a simple but highly effective knowledge management system which, we argue, offers opportunities for tracking, measuring and monitoring knowledge as part of the process. From this basis, we go on to part III of the book to discuss the individual challenges of virtual management.

Case Study *The Open University*

Established in 1969, the Open University (OU) is Britain's largest university, with more than 200,000 students per year (including 45,000 graduate students annually). Its purpose is to provide university degrees through home study rather than through the conventional method of teaching face to face. Originally students came from the UK only, but there are now many students in Europe and overseas (even though the OU concept has been widely copied in other countries).

Courses use a range of teaching media including textbooks, television and radio programmes, audio and video tapes and computer software. Personal contact and support comes through locally based tutors, a network of 330 regional study centres in the UK and overseas, and annual residential schools.

The OU has been in the forefront of adapting technology for use in teaching, starting with television programmes and moving on in the 1990s to the Internet. As of 2002, more than 150 of the OU's 360-plus courses were using the Internet for various features including virtual tutorials and discussion groups, electronic submission (and marking) of assignments, multimedia teaching materials and computer-mediated conferencing. Around 110,000 OU students read more than 170,000 e-mail and computer conference messages each day. Fourteen OU courses are fully delivered via the Internet. OU researchers are continuing to develop new methods of learning delivery such as 'virtual field trips' for science students and an 'Internet stadium' which can be accessed by up to 100,000 people at a time.

The OU is a highly successful example of the employment of intangible capital, and of adding value through virtual organization. The OU is an important university in its own right, with world-class research programmes and centres; its faculties are involved in the creation and dissemination of knowledge on a number of levels. The value-added comes through the delivery system, which allows students to study for a degree and enhance their own knowledge in qualifications without having to give up work or leave home. Nationally, the OU adds value by increasing the pool of skilled and qualified people, reaching out to people whom the conventional universities cannot attract; for individual students, the OU adds value by enriching their lives, increasing their qualifications and enhancing their earning power by providing them with knowledge.

Source: http://www.open.ac.uk

7 The knowledge transformation process

The previous two chapters have discussed what intangible capital is and some of the ways it is used and valued. What should be clear by now is that all intangible capital is based on knowledge. Knowledge capital itself represents the stocks of knowledge that an organization and its members have to draw on. Human capital consists in the skills, creativity and general ability of the organization's people to transform this knowledge into value-creating or value-adding assets. And finally, organization capital consists in the systems, cultures, processes and so on that facilitate the management and use of knowledge.

But in the end, everything boils down to knowledge itself. Whether managers can use knowledge to create and add value – and particularly in ways where both present and future value can be demonstrated, the central problematique of chapter 6 – depends on how well they can manage knowledge.

Today, knowledge management is becoming a recognized sub-discipline within management in its own right. There is a growing body of literature on the subject; IT journals are increasingly turning to discussions of technological systems for managing knowledge, while other journals such as *Knowledge Management Review* focus on the human and behavioural issues associated with knowledge management. We do not propose to go into the details of knowledge management here. Instead, we intend to concentrate on the single process which lies at the heart of all knowledge management, and which converts the raw materials of knowledge – acquired data, human analysis and inspiration – into finished value. This we call the knowledge transformation process.

Most non-technical works on knowledge management take a behavioural approach to the subject and consider it in the context of knowledge as action. Nonaka and Takeuchi (1995) for example speak of knowledge 'to some end', and describe the knowledge creation process as 'reflection in action'. Zeleny (2000) suggests that knowledge cannot be separated from doing. This position reflects both practicality and pragmatism.

But as we have noted, knowledge is not the same as agency, and to add value to a business's activities, knowledge needs to be employed. Before it can be so used, however, it first needs to be acquired or created, and then very often it needs to be stored until it can be used. This chain of activities makes up the knowledge transformation process. In earlier work (see Warner and Witzel 1998), we have argued that this process is one of the main tasks of the general manager in every organization. The knowledge transformation process begins at the meta-firm level, at which knowledge is acquired or created, and it is the general manager who must take a strategic view of this part of the process. Operationally, the general manager is then directly responsible for ensuring that management is handled and shaped to achieve maximum utility within the firm. Finally, the general manager needs to be able to work at the level of each individual firm function to ensure that knowledge is disseminated for use both within the firm and outside it. Each of these levels is now discussed in more detail.

Let us look for a moment at the implications of this for management in virtual organizations. There are two aspects to virtual organizations that concern us here. One is the idea, noted already at several points in this text, that virtual organizations are more strongly dependent on intangible capital – and therefore on knowledge – than conventional organizations. This tends to be true for the products and services they produce and deliver, but is especially true in terms of their operating systems and processes, which depend absolutely on the circulation of knowledge through technological networks. And second, the nature of management in virtual organizations tends to be less specialized and more general in nature. In chapter 1 we described virtual organizations as being fuzzy and low on structure, with fewer distinctions between jobs and functions, and in chapters 1 and 4 we discussed how workers and managers in virtual organizations needed to take more and broader managerial responsibility for their own work. We will go on to explore this idea in more detail in part III of this book, especially in chapter 8, in which we argue that much of virtual management is general management transferred into a different style of organization. For the present, though, it is important to note that management in virtual organizations requires more and broader knowledge on the part of the manager.

In particular, knowledge management becomes the task of every manager and indeed every worker. It is even possible that all virtual working is in effect 'managerial', in that it involves the management and manipulation of knowledge. The employee in a knowledge-based occupation now has more information than ever, thanks to the applications of the new technology he or she may now have at their disposal. However, the term 'managerial' here may only be relative; the superordinate of the employee may have meta-level information at a higher strategic level than he or she normally has. While empowerment may have taken place in recent years, it is advisable not to overestimate the degree of this.

Figure 7.1 The role of the knowledge transformation process

Inputs (knowledge)

→

Knowledge transformation process

→

Outputs (value)

Regardless of this, it is certainly fair to say that in a virtual organization, the knowledge transformation process is shared by everyone. It is the task of management to make sure that this process is carried out smoothly, efficiently and effectively in a manner that creates and adds value.

The three stages of knowledge transformation

The knowledge transformation process is a simple concept that allows managers to view how knowledge makes the transition from knowledge inputs to value outputs. The process has three stages: knowledge creation and acquisition, knowledge organization and storage, and knowledge use.

Knowledge creation and acquisition

Knowledge acquisition and creation is the stage where knowledge inputs are collected together. The effective acquisition of knowledge by the firm is the core focus of concepts such as Senge's (1990) 'learning organization' developed only a decade or so ago. This facility in turn is built on earlier concepts such as feedback loops developed by Argyris and Schön (1978) and earlier by Forrester (1961). Learning organizations learn through a variety of methods: environmental scanning, prospecting for new sources of information and analysing their own operations for information that can be fed back and increase the organizational stock of knowledge. The difference between the learning organization and earlier forms is that instead of information gathering being a 'staff' or specialist function, it is now conceived of as a whole organization function. In this sense, we may be witnessing a 'qualitative' change in the nature of organizations. While it is difficult to put a precise date on the onset of this phenomenon, it is clear that it occurred in the train of the so-called IT revolution of the last two decades. The emphasis on such 'learning' is only recent and we must in turn wait for its elaboration as a viable organizational concept.

Nonaka and Takeuchi (1995) added a new layer to this idea when distinguishing, following Polanyi (1958), between 'tacit' and 'explicit' knowledge. Explicit knowledge is easy to learn and codify, while tacit knowledge is inherent in individuals and much more difficult to codify and transmit. The way systems are evolving currently, codification of explicit knowledge may be overtaking the tacit form. There is a need, they say, to draw out tacit knowledge and make it explicit by learning from each other within the organization. There may be a positive 'synergy' in this learning process, to the mutual benefit of the employee and the organization.

And of course, many large companies create knowledge explicitly as well, with R&D functions that rival traditional universities. In cases such as computing

Figure 7.2   The information-gathering function as a spectrum

Specialist . . . . Organizational technology and applications, for example, multinational firms like Microsoft not only conduct basic research in-house, but have also set up large research centres in university cities such as Cambridge in the UK and make substantial grants to university departments. IBM spends more on scientific research than many universities, with research centres in both North America and Europe, and its staff have already won a Nobel Prize (for the development of the scanning-tunnelling microscope in 1987). Firms working in pharmaceuticals and material sciences are also deeply involved in scientific research. Nor is research limited to tangible research; there is also much intangible research into areas such as systems management. In fact, the distinction between created and acquired knowledge is seldom clear-cut: even the most advanced innovation and research builds on stocks of knowledge that have often been acquired or learned from other sources.

As noted in chapter 2, Nonaka and Takeuchi develop a fourfold methodology for the creation and acquisition of knowledge. The four methods are socialization, externalization, combination and internalization.

- Socialization is a means of sharing and expanding tacit knowledge. Nonaka and Takeuchi describe it as 'a process of sharing experiences and thereby creating tacit knowledge such as shared mental models and technical skills. An individual can acquire tacit knowledge directly from others without using language' (1995:62–63). Tacit knowledge is created in this way through shared experiences; the authors note that it is very difficult for socialization of knowledge to occur unless participants in a process are able to draw on and pass on their own experiences to others. As vehicles for this kind of learning and knowledge creation, Nonaka and Takeuchi cite the 'brainstorming camps' set up by Honda and other Japanese companies which bring people together through various mental – and even physical – exercises so that they create a shared mental model.

- Externalization converts 'tacit knowledge into explicit concepts. It is a quintessential knowledge-creation process in that tacit knowledge becomes explicit, taking the shapes of metaphors, analogies, concepts, hypotheses or models' (1995:66). Reflection upon previously acquired knowledge and analysis of concepts creates models, often in the form of metaphors, which become shared mental property. This allows links to be created between concepts that may at first appear to have nothing in common: 'this creative, cognitive process continues as we think of the similarities among concepts and feel an imbalance, inconsistency, or contradiction in their associations, thus often leading to the discovery of new meaning or even to the formation of a new paradigm' (1995:67).

- Combination, as the name suggests, involves the bringing together of different forms and types of explicit knowledge and combining them to make, in effect, new knowledge. Nonaka and Takeuchi describe it as 'a process of systematizing concepts into a knowledge system' (1995:67). This kind of knowledge occurs in many types of research and training; the authors give the example of formal business education such as MBA programmes as an example of knowledge combination in practice. Combination is what we most often do when we learn or acquire knowledge from other sources.

- Lastly, internalization 'is a process of embodying explicit knowledge into tacit knowledge. It is closely related to "learning by doing"' (1995:68). This is a complex and time-consuming process, the main aim of which is often to allow employees to empathize with or better understand the experiences of others (fellow employees, customers etc.). It can also be used as a reinforcing device for corporate culture. Nonaka and Takeuchi cite again the example of Honda, where the a sort of mythologizing of the corporate founder, Honda Soichiro, has taken place through the medium of biographies and other material about his life and career; the explicit knowledge these create is taken in by employees and managers and becomes part of their own mental models which, shared with others, go to make up Honda's corporate culture.

This methodology is a particularly strong one, as it deals with both tacit and explicit learning and knowledge creation. The examples Nonaka and Takeuchi give show that there are a variety of routes to knowledge creation and acquisition, depending on the nature of the company and the kind of knowledge it seeks on a given occasion. The best knowledge managers will be aware of all four of these methods and will use them all, sometimes in hybrid combinations.

Knowledge organization and storage

Because knowledge – especially tacit knowledge – is intangible, it is difficult to know when it will be needed, or how much; further, there is no way of predicting with certainty how long the required knowledge will take to acquire. A good knowledge management strategy, therefore, seeks to acquire or create knowledge in advance of when it is likely to be needed, rather than trying to develop a 'just-in-time' programme of knowledge acquisition. Although resources must be used carefully to ensure too much effort and resources are not spent on acquiring knowledge that will never be useful, it is generally helpful to err on the side of caution and risk collecting too much knowledge rather than too little. Great innovative organizations such as Hewlett-Packard, Intel, Microsoft, Matsushita and Sony have tended to bring forward their major innovations out of stocks of existing knowledge, rather than defining a product and the setting up a research programme to design it. Such a strategy may be more cost-effective in the short term, but debatable over the long haul.

However, once information is acquired or created it then has to be stored in a fashion so that it can be later recalled and used. The tasks here concern not only the decision on what kinds of knowledge to retain (one of the authors, who spent some years as a local councillor, once drafted a report on local planning issues only to have it rejected by council officers on the grounds that 'it contains too much information'), but also the organization of knowledge storage in such a way that the organization remains aware of what knowledge it has and where to find it when required. The organization thus needs systems for the planning, control, organization and direction of knowledge once it has been created or acquired. The primary need is usually to structure an often inchoate mass of knowledge and put it into forms which are usable within the organization. Planning future knowledge needs and acquisition strategies, co-ordinating knowledge management activities, and costing and paying for knowledge management are all included here. These necessary steps help keep the knowledge transformation process tightly bound to the firm's own needs and goals.

Knowledge organization also includes storage and dissemination. Frequently knowledge is stored (most commonly in paper files or electronic memory) until its use is required. The human brain is particularly adept at this form of 'just-in-time' knowledge management, holding knowledge in memory until it is required for a certain task and then retrieving it swiftly. We refer to a 'library' of skills that employees may call upon in this domain later, below. Expert knowledge systems can, however, codify these routines.

Knowledge dissemination, the passing on of acquired knowledge to other individuals and organizations, is widely regarded as one of the most difficult tasks. It is one of the primary focuses of Nonaka and Takeuchi in their 'hypertext organization' model; they regard the dissemination, rather than the acquisition of knowledge as critical to competitive advantage. Dissemination may take place not only within organizations but also between them. Dissemination must take place in a form that keeps transaction costs (see Coase 1937) both within the firm and within, say, a network, to the minimum.

Knowledge use

The end result of the knowledge transformation process is the employment of knowledge in such a way as to benefit either the individual possessing it, the firm more generally, or both. In most literature on knowledge in business contexts the use of knowledge is considered primarily in terms of R&D and innovation. Doing this ignores the fact that knowledge is in use and circulation in every part of a firm every day. Production facilities depend on knowledge to produce products and services required by the customer; marketers depend absolutely on customer knowledge to achieve success. All this is part and parcel of the value-creation process, as described in chapter 6. The key to knowledge use lies in having pre-generated stocks of knowledge on hand which are suitable for use, and which are organized and stored in such a way that knowledge assets can be easily retrieved and disseminated. That, in our view, is one of the primary functions of knowledge management.

The knowledge transformation process: some issues

The knowledge transformation process goes on every day in every firm, but it is little understood. One of the problems that has been encountered since the beginning of the Industrial Revolution is the confusion of knowledge itself with the technology needed to support knowledge-based tasks. This has led, for example, to knowledge dissemination being largely handled by IT departments, which are not always well-equipped for the task. Additionally, as the references above point out, technology does not create virtual space, but simply enhances and extends it. Knowledge acquisition, too, has suffered from over-specialization. Knowledge creation has often been locked up inside R&D departments, while wider knowledge acquisition has been the province of training and HR managers; only recently have we begun seeing moves towards making managers, and sometimes staff more generally, responsible for their own knowledge acquisition and empowered to develop their own training plans.

Knowledge management has rarely been considered in anything other than piecemeal fashion; this may be considered as a major drawback analytically. The classical economists, when they defined the division of labour, *pari passu* defined the division of knowledge, and over the succeeding two centuries that division has, if anything, been reinforced. It is true that they sought to 'represent' reality analytically as they saw it, but since what they found was also perceived as 'normative', this hardly helped. The scientific management movement in the last century, with its emphasis on functionalism, further promoted the compartmentalization and separation of knowledge; knowledge use tasks have become tightly defined and focused on specific aspects of a process, product or service. But with the so-called IT revolution, we can now see that a qualitative systemic and organizational change may be taking place.

One of the aims of business process re-engineering has been to break down these barriers (Hammer and Champy 1993; Davenport 1993), and for all its excesses, the BPR movement has at least been successful in forcing managers to think more about processes and less about tasks. This emphasis in turn has broadened the scope of the knowledge use tasks required of the individual manager and employee. The related trend towards team-based working has had some of the same effects. By having to think further up and down the line of production, managers and employees have to develop a larger personal library of skills they can pull out and use when demanded. Each employee's library may be seen as an intangible capital asset, both to him or herself, as well

Figure 7.3 Library of skills

Inputs

↓

'Library' of skills

↓

Internalization/externalization process

↓

Outputs

as to the organization for which they work. The acquisition of the library may take years to accumulate, heavily drawing on social capital. Since it is portable, firms may try to minimize employee mobility.

This library may be correspondingly internalized or externalized. The individual worker or manager may actually possess the skills, but equally may not. It is important that they know where to find the tools demanded by the task; for example, which software programme to use for a specific purpose, which menu to use, what the menu items' functions are and so on. Managers may be able to implement X or Y technique, but they may also need to call upon externalized management skills (such as an HRM package for selection or appraisal). Many of these packages may be bought 'off the shelf', although some may need to be customized. It is this externalization that will, in our opinion, increasingly characterize virtual organization and its management. The balance between the internalization and externalization processes may, however, be one of the significant dilemmas of HRM in this new form of organizational life.

From the above discussion, we may conclude that the learning organization has become a reality in recent years, and that a shift from a specialist to a whole-organization function has occurred in organizations as they have become increasingly virtual. Employees have a personal library of skills upon which they can call, and this may take both internalized and externalized forms.

Knowledge transformation in virtual organizations

We have described this process at length because the knowledge transformation process lies at the heart of management in virtual organizations. The acquisition, dissemination and use of knowledge in these organizations is not an occasional occurrence. It happens constantly; it is at the heart of all communications, all networks, indeed all business processes. At the same time, the lack of physical proximity and the fuzzy nature of virtual organization make all these processes additionally complex. Processes such as socialization and externalization, for example, traditionally happen when groups of people come together. They can be – and are – managed virtually, but they require three things: higher levels of technical and learning skills, a willingness in individuals to take more responsibility for their own learning and to learn proactively, rather than being guided by a facilitator, and the necessary effort of imagination to conceive of a virtual learning community, such as a virtual camp or virtual classroom, and to work and participate in it.

One of the most important tasks of the manager in the virtual organization is to keep the transformation process going on, on a constant and continuous basis. Inefficiencies in the knowledge transformation process in these organizations have serious consequences. First, if there is no knowledge to be transmitted, communications networks begin to fail. When this happens, employees working remotely begin to lose touch. They can become demotivated; they may continue to work willingly, but their efforts could be valueless thanks to lack of co-ordination and focus; in extreme cases they may go beyond the ethical and moral boundaries of the organization and begin acting dangerously (to the organization) or even criminally. Nick Leeson's career at Barings could not have ended as it did had there been proper flow of knowledge from his desk to his head office in London. And correspondingly, as the centre of an organization loses touch with its outlying units, it lacks the information it needs to monitor, co-ordinate, plan and structure. And the value it adds for customers begins to decline.

Conclusion

We have discussed the knowledge transformation process as a task of the virtual general manager. We will go further, and say that it is probably the single central task on which all other tasks of management in virtual organization depend. The present chapter only reinforces the point that the knowledge transformation process is the 'motor' of the virtual organization. What those tasks are forms the subject of part III of this book. We begin by restating the view that virtual management is also becoming general management, and that the successful virtual manager is someone who is also a successful general manager. What general management is and what its relationship to virtual management is are discussed in the next chapter.

Case Study *Buckman Laboratories*

Buckman Laboratories is an international chemical company based in Memphis, Tennessee. It has eight factories in various locations around the world, producing speciality chemical products. Although turnover is US$270 million annually, the company has few employees dispersed over a wide area; 1200 staff in 80 countries. Buckman uses a virtual knowledge network called K'Netix to link all its employees and to create and share knowledge. Staff refer to K'Netix as a 'knowledge forum' and regard it as the central feature of the company's culture.

Bob Buckman, the company's CEO, has created a culture in which staff are encouraged to be as close to the customer as possible. This means getting out of the office and travelling frequently in order to visit customers. The other side of the coin is that staff have less face-to-face contact with each other, and frequently work on their own. The K'Netix system is the means by which they maintain contact and share ideas.

Buckman Laboratories believes that knowledge-sharing not only empowers employees and makes them better able to do their jobs, but creates synergies that make the whole company more effective. Not only employees but also customers have access to the system, and can talk to each other across the globe. One common use for the system is problem-solving; a customer can log onto K'Netix asking for technical help with a particular problem or issue –

▶

not only Buckman employees, but also other customers can write back with ideas and suggestions. If competitive issues are involved, however, the system also allows Buckman to create private forums where customers can speak confidentially to the company about their needs and how to solve them.

The K'Netix system not only allows Buckman to function on several levels as a virtual organization, but it also allows the company and its customers to generate, store and use knowledge to add value. In the Buckman approach, the virtual organization and the knowledge organization are nearly synonymous.

Source: 'Buckman Labs is Nothing But Net' *The Fast Manager* (2002), www.Fastcompany/online/03/buckman.html.

Managing in virtual organizations

8   The general manager

The last few years have seen a renewed growth in interest in 'general management'. In part, this interest has been driven by the emergence of fuzzy, decentralized organizational forms such as the virtual organization. With slimmed-down headquarters and dispersed operating units, these new organizational types no longer have large managerial structures. With fewer managers, there is both less need for functional specialization and less opportunity to practise it. Managers have to become generalists, in outlook and in practice. They have to be capable of moving from one task to another, and even of managing multiple, variant tasks simultaneously. Above all, perhaps, the ability to conceptualize and 'imagineer' a large network and one's own place in it requires managers who are able to view the larger picture and use holistic and multi-functional models for the organization as a whole and their own work.

We suggest that rather than inventing an entirely 'new' form of management called virtual management, it is preferable to adapt an existing management model, general management, to the challenges of operating in a virtual world. There are two advantages to this. First, reconfiguring the existing general management model creates a type of management that is capable of managing both conventional and virtual assets in a simultaneous way. In earlier chapters we suggested that all virtual organizations require at least some conventional components, including technology, the artefacts that enable virtual organization, and people, who provide the imagination that drives it. This implies that a mix of virtual and conventional assets, rather than a 'pure' virtual organization, will always be required, although the nature of that mix will depend on the situation, the organization, and its goals and strategy. This mix will be the subject of chapter 9. Second, the existing general-management model has a number of strengths, on which virtual management can draw. Elsewhere we have implied that managing in virtual organizations requires the addition of new management skills to existing ones, not the substitution of new skills for old. This chapter looks at the concept of general management, describing the overall idea and then breaking it down into a series of practical tasks. In chapter 10, we return to this model and show how it can be adapted to managing in virtual organizations, once the strategic decision about the virtual/real mix has been decided upon.

What is general management?

Early theories of management, such as the school of scientific management developed by Frederick Winslow Taylor and his colleagues (Taylor 1911; Warner 2001), concentrate largely on line management and tended therefore to divide management into functions. 'Shop' management, what we would call operations management, was seen as quite separate from the management of other business functions such as marketing, sales, accounting and finance and so on. Despite considerable criticism from those who believed that management should take a broader perspective of the organization as a whole (Emerson 1913; Fayol 1917; Follett 1937), this idea of management persisted until after the Second World War.

In a number of important contributions starting in the 1950s, Peter Drucker (1954, 1967) argued that managers should be capable of taking a broad view of their organizations. His philosophy of 'management by objectives' began a trend away from scientific management, a trend that in some circles even became a backlash. Increasingly, the focus of management was placed on human elements. Whereas under scientific management the primary managerial task was control, increasingly under the influence of Drucker it became leadership. Managers were no longer 'overseers' but inspired 'creative' thinkers and 'catalysts' for action in their firms. These ideas have proved very difficult to implement; for a long time firms were, not surprisingly, reluctant to let go of the certainty provided by controls and enter the creative and co-ordinative world envisioned by people such as Drucker; recently, however, some managers have begun to escape their functional boxes and become true generalists. HR development has begun to focus on providing broad experience and education for managers, emphasizing leadership, strategy and vision rather than technical skills. Business schools reacted to these changes by sharpening up their MBA and other programmes in the late 1980s. The general-management model is now widely employed by large companies, who continue to rely on functional specialists (and, increasingly, on 'expert systems') to provide control, but who may also use experienced and talented generalists to provide leadership and vision at the top (Kotter 1990).

General management as a universalist and normative approach can imply a focus on the basic managerial task regardless of context. Drucker, for example, has been accused of promoting the development of 'transferable managers', able to do the same job in any firm regardless of setting by virtue of their basic management skills. However, there remain distinctive cultural differences in the general-management model around the world. In the US, general management is seen as being primarily a process-driven task, wherein the primary responsibility is to manage the process by which products are created and delivered to the market. The task of senior general managers is to ensure that this process is carried out. Leadership and communications skills are thus very important qualifications for any management post (see Heller 2001).

In Europe, on the other hand, general management still has a strong technical orientation (with the possible exception of the UK, which has been more strongly influenced by the US). For example, general managers in German companies often rise from scientific or engineering backgrounds. They are more likely to have PhDs in a technical discipline than their US counterparts, and they are also less likely to have postgraduate management qualifications (Warner 1987). Indeed, the entire German and for that matter Central and North European management and vocational training system tends to differ from the Anglo-American model in this relative emphasis on technical, task-related goals. In Southern Europe there is still a strong social cohesiveness. Here, as in the past, general managers in many large firms continue to be chosen from the same family or social groups as the company's founder or leader. European management also tends to be more hierarchical than in other regions, although paradoxically European general managers can also be more interventionist and less likely to encourage entrepreneurship among subordinates.

Much the same phenomenon has been observed in Japan, where training systems have been influenced by those of Germany. Japanese general managers tend to be a socially cohesive group; firms tend to recruit their managers from the same university, for example, and the top people in organizations tend to have very similar backgrounds and education. The bottom-up structure of many Japanese companies, it is said, means that Japanese general managers spend more time concentrating on long-term vision and strategy than on direct management of processes, although others have characterized Japanese firms as being strongly hierarchical but with a longer time horizon (Fruin 1992).

In the mid-1970s, Drucker (1974) argued that managers in fact play a central role both within the firm and in the market. It was a very clear statement of how he saw management, not just in terms of specifics but a magisterial perspective, bold and far-reaching, rare amongst writers on organization. Their principal purpose, he said, is the stimulation and satisfaction of market demand. In order to do this, managers must be capable of managing the entire company and must be able to use all its resources in the most efficient and effective manner. They must therefore be masters of all business disciplines, from finance and operations to marketing and HRM. They need to know accounting and cost control, the psychology of consumer behaviour, IT, corporate structure and performance analysis and environmental management. In additional to these kinds of functional knowledge, however, the general manager must also have two further abilities: the ability to develop a vision of the company and its future, and the ability to transmit that vision to subordinates and to motivate them to achieve the company's goals. This ability to translate vision into action, sometimes referred to as entrepreneurship, has become one of the most prized of all corporate qualities (Drucker 1974).

The 1980s were sometimes characterized as the era of the 'lone wolf', when corporate raiders and talented entrepreneurial individuals were able to make a strong impact on the business world. By contrast, the 1990s have been described as the era of the network, when managers and even companies have begun to band together for survival. The reasons for this shift may be partly ascribed to faster technological change and partly as a response to greater environmental complexity. The twin influences of IT and globalization proved to be decisive shapers of how management was to emerge. Crucial managerial skills in this new era include teamwork, networking and alliance building and, perhaps most important of all, mastery of information technology. These skills are likely to become ever more important in the future, as it becomes increasingly clear that only very rare and talented individuals can master all the challenges of general management. A team approach, with team members chosen on the basis of particular complementary competencies, was seen as one of way of overcoming this problem. Team-based decisions are likely to be based on a greater breadth of information, and thus are correspondingly less risky. They also allow for greater creativity and can help overcome the problems of the 'machine bureaucracy' (Den Hertog and Tolner 2001).

By the mid-1990s, it was widely recognized that businesses needed to be more responsive, to react more quickly to change in their environments. There was a growing realization that too great an emphasis had been placed on 'control' and 'structure' rather than 'autonomy' and 'flexibility' in the way organizations had been run. This analysis represented a return to a 'general management' or 'strategic' perspective. A move towards looking at things more 'holistically' was 'in the air'.

There was also continuing pressure on managers to learn from other cultures and adopt new approaches to their task. Global markets were no longer the preserve of a single business culture. The 'North American' model was no longer *de rigueur*. A comparative approach to management began increasingly to attract attention. The rise of the Asian tiger economies pointed to the emergence of new management models; the temporary collapse of these economies in the late 1990s was due more to structural factors than to any defects in management models, and the Asian management model continues to thrive. The economic revolution now taking place in China, with the People's Republic of China predicted to achieve the status of an economic superpower in the century just begun, has a managerial counterpart as Chinese managers educated in a centrally planned economy heavily influenced by scientific management struggle to cope with the transition to Western ways of doing business (Chen 1995; Warner 1999). While it is too early to see the emergent Chinese Big Business as a serious 'global' player yet (see Nolan 2001), it has attracted more and more attention from management researchers.

Accordingly, Parikh (1991) has suggested that Western managers can learn much from their Eastern counterparts in terms of philosophy and approach. Eastern values and attributes such as greater spatial awareness and a Confucian sense of obligation may have something to offer to the beleaguered general manager in the Western-based multinational. So large has this field grown that according to one recent account, the number of books and articles on cross-cultural management is now to be numbered in the tens of thousands (see Warner and Joynt 2002). It is clear that the general manager of the future will not only be 'internationalized' in terms of his or her awareness of markets and managements, but also attuned to cross-cultural cues, signs and symbols in the global marketplace. In order to learn these, rotation around the functional departments of the corporation will no longer be enough; cross-cultural experi-ence will have to join cross-functional experience.

Perhaps most critical, though, is the search for new directions. Drucker (1995), looking back over recent management trends such as benchmarking, total quality management and re-engineering, remarks that the central challenge is not to develop more 'how to do' tools, but to determine 'what to do'. He concludes that in many cases of business failure, the problem is not that the wrong things are being done, but that the right things are being done fruitlessly; this, he says, is because the 'assumptions on which the organization has been built and is being run no longer fit reality' (Drucker 1995:95). It is this search for a 'reality fit' that preoccupies many managers and many firms today, and general managers are probably the only people who can find this fit for their organizations. Recognizing this leads us to a new appreciation of the organic links between organizations and general management. As ever-faster technological change and ever-growing environmental complexity and indeed, uncertainty, present critical challenges to today's managers, the search for a new 'paradigm' becomes increasingly pressing.

Why functional management?

Why did management, in the era of scientific management, become so specialist-oriented, and why has it taken so long to claw our way back to a more general concept of what management should be?

Organizations begin as dyads. From the perspective of the classical economists, firms are at their very essence two-way partnerships between capitalist and labourer. From the very outset, however, by recognizing the division of labour, Adam Smith – and by extension all those who came after him – recognized the

Figure 8.1   The growth of organizational hierarchy

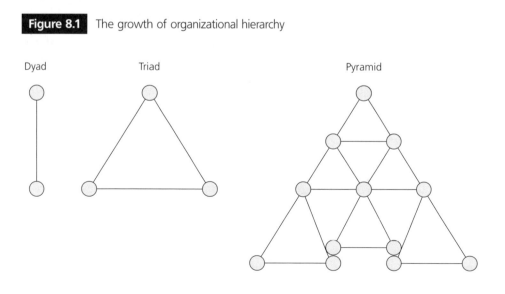

Dyad   Triad   Pyramid

managerial role that capital must also play. Indeed, it may be that general management has been the principal continuity in the evolution of the Western firm down through the ages. The dyad becomes a triad as soon as the number of labourers exceeds the number of capitalists. If the number of labourers grows quickly or to a large size, as it did in many firms during the Industrial Revolution, then the triad becomes a pyramid (see figure 8.1).

Organizationally, then, early firms existed as pyramids. The height of the pyramid and the steepness of the slope varied from culture to culture, but fundamentally the same model applied. At the top is the controller of capital; at the bottom are the suppliers of labour. Liberal and classical economic thought assigned to the capitalist the role of director and controller of both capital and labour, without bothering to ascertain whether the suppliers of capital actually played that role; indeed, the classical economists dismiss this distinction as unimportant. And, on one level, it is not. The task of guiding and controlling the firm is again more or less the same whether the manager is also the owner or not. There are many other variables – internal organization, culture, product sector, firm size, position in the life-cycle, the skill of the individual managers – which will have far greater impact on the governance of the firm (Heller and Wilpert 1979).

Essentially, professional managers are employed for one of two reasons: either the owners of capital voluntarily abrogate control, or the organization reaches a size that the owners can no longer control it unaided (a combination of the two is also possible). In the second case, there appear to be three reasons why firms need to take on professional salaried managers from outside the circle of the owner and his or her immediate family:

- when the firm locates operations at a considerable distance from headquarters, making direct daily control impossible;
- when the firm requires additional technical expertise and knowledge;
- when the firm's financial affairs reach a sufficient size and complexity that they require dedicated personnel to manage them.

Thus there is no single factor which determines the separation of ownership and control. In fact, such separation ought correctly to be seen as a part of growth stages of the firm's life-cycle. The form that separation takes is dependent on the variables noted above. Different cultures, for example, influence the separation in different ways. In Anglo-American cultures, M-form businesses such as Chandler (1962) describes put large distances between ownership and control, although one does not have to look too hard to find exceptions to this rule. (It is interesting to note that in one early text in the scientific management tradition, Parsons [1909] actually assumed a conflation of ownership and management. Defining administration as the motive power of the organization, he writes: 'Its source is the ownership-control, the basis of the organization, and from that source this power must be transmitted through the person of the general manager...' [Parsons 1909:30].) German and other North European businesses, too, have tended to establish gaps between ownership and control. In the south of Europe, however, family and personal control remain important in many large firms.

The French tyre firm Michelin, one of the three largest firms in this sector world-wide, is still managed from the top by a fifth-generation family member, and other similar examples abound. Similarly, in the Chinese-influenced business cultures of East Asia, we find ownership and control of large firms to be very closely linked (Chen 1995).

Why did the classical economists, having recognized its importance, not formulate a theory of general management? The answer is probably quite simple: they were not interested. Economists tend to focus on macro-forces, and the role of the individual firm is of limited interest. Alfred Marshall once compared the relationship of the individual business to an industry as being like the relationship of an individual tree to a forest, intimating that firms are by nature ephemeral and transitory (Marshall 1890). The management of firms was largely assumed within their economic structure. Modern theories of 'functional' management did not grow out of this structural milieu, however. Instead, they grew out of a set of quite different circumstances in late nineteenth-century America. The major differences were twofold: first, the Industrial Revolution in America was much more rapid and happened over a much larger geographical space than in Britain; and second, this was now the age of science. Scientific values pervaded all parts of society; the late Victorian period was a time of a passion for measurement, for systems, for order. Frederick Winslow Taylor's great achievement was to adapt the principles of science to the governance of firms, which were at the same time growing at such a rate as to require ever larger numbers of professional managers, for the reasons outlined above. Without scientific management, the new large American firms would probably have evolved much like their European counterparts, in an *ad hoc* fashion with a mix of managerial styles. It is entirely likely that they would not have been as successful as they in fact were.

Thus, the real nature of the managerial revolution in the late nineteenth and early twentieth centuries was that it formalized and promoted the concepts of functional management and management by process. The military/ecclesiastical-derived models that had served Europe up to this point were replaced by models derived directly from the new science (and indeed it was not long before the term 'management science' began to appear) based on systems. But the era of functional management is now coming to an end. The need for generalists, and general managers, is now well recognized. Today's general managers, properly trained and equipped with information and decision systems, can function better and faster than their functional counterparts, thanks to a broader and more holistic view of organizations, a focus on processes leading to goals rather than processes alone, and a concept of efficiency and effectiveness that embraces the whole business and not just individual tasks.

Of course, making general managers effective in this way requires two major changes in current thinking. First it requires a different approach to training and educating general managers. Mintzberg (1989) has very effectively pointed out the flaws in current management training, arguing that many business schools are still trying to train administrators and not leaders, and that management education is too often superficial and too far removed from the realities of business. The solution may be to develop ways of 'growing' general managers over the long term, probably within the context of a single firm or group of firms. Practical experience, in quantity, can be seen as a very important aspect of such training. Here also, in a modern context, the model used by Japanese firms, and also some Chinese family businesses, both of which tend to groom managers within the organization, using on-the-job training and giving prospective managers solid practical experience on the shop floor before promoting them through the ranks, may be relevant (Chen 1995).

Second, and more difficult, this way of thinking also involves rethinking the firm, and in particular the relationship between the manager and the worker, and also between the firm and its owners. Hands-on management almost certainly means bringing all parties closer together and blurring the distinctions between them. There are many antecedents for this, stretching back across the centuries. Schumpeter, in his work on the entrepreneur, has suggested that entrepreneurship and management are intrinsically linked (Schumpeter 1934). As examples, we have the management system developed by Tomas Bata and also the early and visionary views of Henry Ford (Ford 1926). Again too there are examples from East Asia, such as the *ringi* system prevalent in Japanese companies. We need to be less concerned with developing rigid models of management and more with what the Japanese again call *wakon yosei* (Japanese values, Western knowledge) wherein cross-cultural adaptation takes place in order to achieve fitness for purpose, rather than fit with preconceived ideas (Warner 1984). These are all possibilities; there may well be others.

What general managers do

So, what does all this mean for management in virtual organizations? In fact, if we compare the nature of virtual organizations as described in earlier chapters with the nature of general management as summarized above, we see a number of parallelisms, for example:

- both require a broad and holistic view of the organization and its environment;
- both are concerned with setting strategies and meeting goals rather than the minute management of tasks and processes;
- both have the co-ordination of the efforts of others towards meeting goals as a central focus;
- both place strong emphasis on the human factors in organization, and less on organizational structure and hierarchy – indeed, both can be said to transcend hierarchy;
- both depend on communications to achieve co-ordination;
- both have a strong focus on knowledge – in particular, both require the accumulation of stocks of knowledge capital across a broad range of subjects. In terms of general management, this is inherent in the need for generalists who can manage across a broad spectrum of issues and challenges.

The connections become even more apparent when we set out what it is that general managers actually do. Because general management is necessarily a fuzzy discipline in which results count for more than procedures, it is correspondingly difficult to define what exactly general managers do on a daily basis, and few authors have made any attempt to do so. One of the few is the French management theorist Henri Fayol, who in 1917 set out his ideas on management in a way that focused on the whole organization and not on the specialist functions of Taylorist scientific management. Fayol divided management into seven separate sets of tasks, which are generally known by the acronym POSDCORB:

- planning;
- organizing;
- staffing;
- directing;
- co-ordinating;
- reporting;
- budgeting.

The Fayol model has had many critics (Barnard 1938; Mintzberg 1989), who charge that Fayol too has reduced management to a series of functions. But it is important not to see the tasks as mutually exclusive. Fayol himself did not see it this way; he devised this classification in the belief that all management tasks could, even if at the most basic level, fit into one of these seven categories. But he did not believe in specialist managers looking after each of the seven; rather, he argued that all of the seven were in some way part of the task of every manager.

Fayol's theory has its imperfections, but it remains the best simple description and classification of the daily tasks and duties of management yet developed. Below, we summarize each in turn and its implications for managers.

Planning

Planning is about deciding where the organization will go. More detailed tasks here include information gathering and analysis, forecasting in both macro and micro terms, formulating goals, setting out strategies for meeting those goals and communicating those goals to others in the organization. The latter three processes can be as simple or as complicated as the organization chooses to make them. They can be directive and top-down, or they can be consultative and bottom-up; in the French original Fayol uses the term *prévoyance*, which has connotations of foresight and anticipation of needs rather than directive planning *per se*. No matter how the process works, however, the need to carry out these tasks in some form remains a management imperative. The first task of management, therefore, is to give the organization directive.

Organizing

The Harvard business historian Alfred Chandler (1962) commented that 'structure follows strategy', and perhaps not by coincidence the second element in the Fayol scheme is organization. The tasks of organization are focused on how to ensure the best possible fit between the structure of the business and its goals, what Miles and Snow (1978) call 'organizational fitness for purpose'. Tasks here include defining not only the physical structures of the organization but also its communications networks, its knowledge management system and the personal and intangible relationships that go to make up concepts such as corporate culture. Thus the tasks of structure are both operational and human-centred. They are the sole province of neither the HRM department nor the operating departments; they concern the organization as a whole.

Staffing

Staffing tasks ensure first that the right people are in the right jobs, and second that people's full potential is available to the organization. Traditional functional organizations hand over sole responsibility for staffing to the HRM department, but in the Fayol scheme, responsibility for staff rests with every manager. Today, staffing tasks include many of the tasks we might also associate with leadership, such as organizing and leading teams, motivating people and providing support for junior managers and employees at every level. Staffing is of critical importance in every organization.

Directing

Again, directing is often pigeonholed as a 'leadership' function, but in reality every manager has some responsibility for this. Again too, the word 'direction' can be applied in many ways. The manager can literally direct or order his or her subordinates to carry out tasks; but he or she can also provide direction for the latter through example, precept, learning and other methods which enable employees to understand more clearly what the organization needs of them, what their own place in the organization is and how best they can carry out their own tasks. Motivation, rather than direction, might be a better word for this set of tasks, which also have close relations with the staffing tasks described above.

Co-ordinating

Early management theory spoke often about the need for control, but Follett (1937) argued that the only really effective method of control is co-ordination. Effective co-ordination causes things to be done without compelling or ordering people to do them, but rather by harmonizing efforts to that everyone is pulling willingly towards the same goal. Sometimes effective co-ordination requires minimal managerial effort; a good, smoothly running system is one that runs itself with a minimum of intervention. However, continuous managerial supervision and monitoring is required to ensure that the efforts continue to be harmonized. Co-ordinating tasks are particularly suited to network models of organization, where co-ordinators are in close touch with other members of the organization so that information and knowledge can be exchanged easily and quickly.

Reporting

Reporting tasks are those that concentrate on the gathering and dissemination of information and knowledge. In the original scheme, reporting tasks were viewed as important for two reasons: first they provided raw data and information from below to top management to enable the latter to make more informed decisions, and second they ensured fiscal controls. In the modern environment, reporting is an essential set of tasks if transparency and accountability are to be achieved. They thus have implications not only for top management but for other levels of the firm and for stakeholders outside the firm. Reporting tasks have some kinship with the communications tasks we go on to discuss below.

Budgeting and finance

Managers have a responsibility to use their capital wisely, for the benefit of both the organization and its shareholders. Although there are many specialist tasks of budgeting, accounting and corporate finance, at the most basic level every manager participates in the following: the allocation of funds to be spent on particular projects, calculating the potential return on each and then managing finances so that those returns are achieved. This requires managers to be financially literate and to know the financial implications of decisions. Once again, these tasks are common to all managers across all organizations, regardless of organizational form or function.

New tasks for virtual management

The seven tasks are, to repeat, common across all organizations in all ages. However, the additional complexity of managing in virtual organizations requires further sets of tasks to be 'bolted on' to the original model. These four tasks have affinities to some of the tasks above, but they still require new managerial skills and will take up separate proportions of the manager's time. The four new tasks are communication, assessment, learning and valuation, which we refer to the by the acronym CALV.

Communication

Communication consists in ensuring that knowledge flows are efficient and timely, linking all the elements of an organization to each other and to suppliers and customers. Communication is, as noted above, important to the knowledge transformation process and plays a key role in turning knowledge into value. Communication also ensures focus among the disparate parts of the organization, helps ensure employees remain motivated and committed. Management skills required here are a mixture of those required for the directing, co-ordinating and reporting of the tasks mentioned above; it can be seen that managing communications flows is in effect a mixture of all three. Managers in virtual organizations can expect to spend a high proportion of each day involved in communications tasks.

Assessment

Assessment here means the matching of the organization's goals with its form and structure on a dynamic basis, and altering or amending that structure when opportunities arise. It overlaps the planning, organization and staffing skill sets mentioned above. It is listed separately here because the rapidly changing environment in which most virtual organizations operate, plus the highly flexible nature of those organizations, require an ongoing co-ordination of all three elements. Assessment skills include planning – including contingency planning – analysis, forecasting, organizational design and configuration, and team and group leadership.

Learning

Learning here means the constant replenishment of an organization's stock of knowledge capital through such activities as training and education, R&D, environmental scanning and so on. Learning tasks form part of the knowledge transformation process, described in detail in the previous chapter. Learning skills are a key ingredient in all modern management, especially virtual management.

Valuation

Valuation is the continuous and dynamic reassessment of knowledge assets in terms of their present and future value to the firm. This refers not only to fiscal valuation, but also to other and more subjective valuations as described in chapter 6, in which we discussed the inability of conventional book-keeping and accounting methods to measure the value-added and future potential value of intangible capital. The new skills that will need to be developed for this purpose will have to form part of the tool-kit of every manager in every virtual organization.

Conclusion

Fayol qualified his classification of managerial work with the comment that 'there is nothing absolute in management'; 'Seldom do we apply the same principle twice in identical circumstances; allowance must be made for changing circumstances' (Fayol 1917:19). That applies to both the above classifications, POSDCORB and CALV. Managerial work does not consist of carefully routinized sets of tasks formed around these categories; in a given day, it would be impossible for a manager to estimate in advance how much time he or she will spend on each or even, at the end of the day, how much time he or she had spent on each. Task boundaries overrun; a single action can be performed which has implications for multiple tasks. Management never fits into neat pigeonholes such as these.

But classifying tasks in this way has a useful function. It allows us to think about what we are actually doing, and even more, what we may be not doing. Many failures in management can be attributed to ignoring just one of these basic principles. The best plans in the world will not succeed if the structure and staff are not there to support them; the best staff in the world are unlikely to succeed if they are not motivated and co-ordinated to achieve the firm's goals.

This is true of conventionally structured organizations. It is even more true of virtual organizations, for two reasons. First, managerial responsibility is more devolved; each individual in a virtual organization takes at least some managerial responsibility for his or her own work. With a greater proportion of the organization involved in managerial work, the need for management tasks to be carried out efficiently and effectively is correspondingly greater. One of the biggest challenges for senior management when making the transition to virtual organization, therefore, is ensuring this 'devolution' of management goes smoothly, and that people at every level understand their managerial tasks and what is required of them. Second, as we have discussed at several points, there is the reliance on intangible capital and on knowledge transformation to add value. The knowledge dimension is present in all the managerial tasks listed above, old and new. But knowledge on its own is inert; it requires to be managed, to be used, in order to add value. Knowledge is the lifeblood of virtual organizations, and ensuring that knowledge continues to circulate is a primary responsibility of managers in such organizations. We have remarked already on the common-knowledge dimension of both general management and virtual management; it is for this reason that we argue that the conventional general-management model can be adapted and added to to create a basis for virtual management.

The following two chapters look at two aspects of managing in virtual organization and discuss the issues that managers have to face. The first primarily refers to setting up or establishing a virtual organization: what should the mix of virtual and conventional elements be? To some extent this choice continues to confront the virtual manager throughout an organization's successive growth, but the choice is particularly critical in terms of early planning, organization and staffing decisions. The choice of real vs virtual is the subject of chapter 9. Chapter

10 then goes on to look at ongoing management issues, focusing in particular on how managerial and task responsibilities are allocated in virtual environments.

Case Study *NTT DoCoMo*

NTT DoCoMo is a wireless communications company owned by the Japanese telecoms group NTT. Launched six years ago, the company went public in 1998 and has since been one of the star performers of the otherwise moribund Japanese stock market. It dominates the Japanese mobile communications market, and is a major player in the world market. At time of writing, DoCoMo had around 44 million subscribers to its mobile phone service, and employed around 18,000 people worldwide, in Japan, the US, Europe and Brazil.

Although the company offers a number of services, its star attraction is i-mode, a continuous connection mobile Internet service that is rapidly becoming the most popular mobile communications service in Japan. I-mode is also being licensed to a number of overseas partners. Having already risen to a position of leadership in Japan, DoCoMo is now seeking to create further value by going international. However, DoCoMo's international strategy is based on partnerships, not acquisitions. Having identified a potential partner, the company then usually takes a minority stake in that partner's business, but not a position of control. In the first instance this reduces the level of debt required. DoCoMo's technology and managerial expertise are then deployed to ensure the partner venture is a success; this generates revenue and dividend income which help to swell cash flow. DoCoMo believes this strategy gives it the best of both worlds.

I-mode has been successful in large part because it offers convenience for customers and is easy and simple to set up and use. Not only does this technology mean that the Internet is always available and ready for use – there is no need to log on – but DoCoMo also offers i-mode users quality control in terms of the sites it will support. In order to be i-mode accessible, websites need to be supported by the i-mode platform, and this in turn requires DoCoMo's consent. As the company's own website says, 'We also enhance customers' experience by enforcing stringent criteria with respect to available content. This attention to quality ensures that our service supports only the best available websites.'

Not a true virtual organization in many respects, DoCoMo has shown it understands the virtual world and how to leverage its own knowledge capital into value for both customers and shareholders. The company has a high R&D spend, enabling it to transform knowledge into useful technology and services. The end result is a company that has mastered the virtual marketplace – in a conventional way.

Source: NTT websites: see www.nttdocomo.co.jp.

9 Real vs virtual: the strategy mix

The British-born, later US-resident Nobel Prize-winning economist Ronald Coase (1937) famously described the firm as a nexus of contracts. This metaphor can be replicated on a number of different levels. The conceptualization we ourselves present here, for instance, argues that the firm is a nexus of knowledge flows, with technological communications networks enabling people to create value through the knowledge transformation process swiftly over long distances. However, this is not the only dimension on which businesses operate. If firms were only nexuses of knowledge flows, then they all would be virtual firms. In real life, though, the physical world intrudes. The relationship between the real and virtual spaces is as important as the spaces themselves.

It was Coase, too, who suggested that transaction costs determine the boundaries of the firm. Today, technological change in general and the Internet in particular has reduced these costs, thus changing the parameters of organizational change both in time and space. The basic concept of a business organization that recognizes that its knowledge is its primary asset and is able to capitalize on this and create 'competitive advantage' is now widely recognized, even if not always fully understood. There are plenty of examples of companies that have achieved success by doing so. The phenomenal growth of the software industry, with companies such as US-based Lotus and Microsoft, and of telecoms companies such as Japan-based DoCoMo (see the case study in chapter 8) stands as evidence of how knowledge can be transformed and can in turn transform other outputs. More 'traditional' firms such as Shell, Kao and Toyota have also been able to leverage knowledge into competitive advantage, using models of knowledge acquisition and management as described in the earlier chapters. Just as the Industrial Revolution of the eighteenth century led to a new kind of business organization, the large manufacturing firm, so the information revolution of the twentieth is leading to the development of another new form, the knowledge firm. It seems safe to predict that the influence of the knowledge firm on business, society and the global economy will be at least as great as that of the introduction of what became known as the 'factory system'.

From his mid-nineteenth century perspective as a social critic, Karl Marx saw commodified labour as a 'process', with some knowledge components and some physical components (Marx 1933 edn). If we accept this view, we can conceptualize the notion of virtual management and the management of tangible assets as co-existing and complementary, not as opposites. Another way to envisage this might be the 'Daoist dualism', with management of virtual and tangible assets as corresponding to the dark side (ying) and the light side (yang) of the mountain (Clark 2000). In any case, we need to recognize that no organization is fully virtual or fully tangible. Instead, all operate in a kind of 'shadowland' that is composed of both these states, with tangible artefacts (technology) and people supporting, enabling and creating a virtual network of knowledge flows. A dualistic perspective of organization may thus illuminate matters and lead us to a more insightful view of reality.

It follows that if organizations have both virtual and tangible forms, then so does management. It is possible, and may in many cases be desirable, to manage virtually even when the organization is largely conventional in form. Indeed, given that management is largely a knowledge-based activity, it can be argued that all management should be conceptualized as a virtual activity. But this concept too has its limits: for example, the impact of leadership dissipates over geographical distance, and is only partly compensated for by communications technology. Group-working and team-working also tend to be less effective when the group or team members are not in proximity unless there are compensating systems which enable easy communication.

There are possible solutions to this problem, most of them provided by technology. Tele-working has been growing; more and more workers are being organized to work outside the conventional workplace. Tele-conferencing and the use of laptops with video-conferencing capability may help here. Technology can be used to construct virtual groups or teams. Virtual group-working, we would argue, is both theoretically and empirically possible. Technology allows us the option to create a mix of virtual and tangible forms.

The new networks of virtual organization may, as Papows (1999) has described, be able to eliminate some of the problems caused by time, distance and organizational barriers. They can also lead to problems of loss of control, lack of monitoring and supervision, poor compliance and, if the systems do not work, misinformation or disinformation creeping into the network (as the Barings and Sumitomo Banks, among others, found out to their cost in the late 1990s).

While establishing an entirely new, virtual organization may be of benefit in some cases, we argue that in most instances the best solution may well be therefore an organizational hybrid, one capable of achieving closer fit with the organization's stakeholders and goals. The task of management in this hybrid organization would be to manage all of an organization's capital, virtual and tangible, in such a way as to draw closer to those goals. This is no easy task and indeed how precisely to marshal these resources is as yet a moot point.

All firms, we would argue, have a dual nature in that they are made up of components in part physical and in part virtual. Non-virtual components are what economists would see as the traditional factors of production: land, labour and capital. They include physical facilities, plant, stock and also the firm's employees. Virtual components are the firm's intangible assets, or as they have sometimes been described, its intangible capital. They are things which cannot be seen or touched, but are nonetheless present; these include the firm's culture, its reputation and that of its products and brands, and most of all, the knowledge inherent in its people, processes, systems and technologies.

Nor can assets always be strictly classified as virtual or non-virtual. As Adam Smith (1776) was the first to point out, machines have value not just as objects, but also for the knowledge of their makers and designers, which is built into them. It is vitally important, then, not to confuse knowledge itself with the arte-facts that store it or the media that transmit it. People in particular take of both forms. A company needs employees partly for the physical force of labour and partly for the intangible force of knowledge, both qualities which are built into each employee or manager. It is important to know how each quality is used and creates value.

And yet, these two components can hardly be separated. As Zeleny (2000) more recently points out, knowledge is a process. 'Knowledge' and 'knowing' may be conceived of as one and the same thing. Knowledge cannot exist independently; it must be present in some thing, be that a person's mind and memory, a magnetic storage device such as a computer disk, any other piece of technology, printed words on a page and so on. There is a symbiotic link between knowledge and artefacts: knowledge cannot exist independently of artefacts. Furthermore, we may argue that such artefacts have no function unless knowledge is present which will make them work. Without knowledge, they are 'empty vessels'.

The mix may be quite different for different firms, even those in the same industry or sector. An example may help to show this more clearly. In the retail book industry, WHSmith and Amazon.com have chosen two quite different mixes of virtual and non-virtual components in establishing their organizations. The former has adopted what might be termed a 'convenience-store' approach: it makes itself available to customers at several thousand locations in town high streets, shopping malls and railway stations. Originally a British-based newsagent, in fact the first to sell papers on the then expanding numbers of railway stations in the nineteenth century, WHSmith have continued to use roughly the same distribution model, putting a large variety of newspapers, magazines, books and other merchandise – some related to books and some not – on display so that consumers can make a quick choice. Choice and exchange happen quickly and often on the spur of the moment, and the customer's level of involvement is typically very low. To reflect this low involvement, WHSmith has a high physical presence, with a large number of physical facilities, high levels of stock and large numbers of staff. Across the Atlantic, Amazon.com, on the other hand, using the Internet, requires a higher level of involvement from customers, who are less likely to browse and more likely to go to the website with a set of specific requirements already in mind. Because of this, Amazon.com has been able to reduce its physical presence, partially substituting physical facilities and staff for virtual systems deployed over the Internet. Yet it still retains a visible and tangible form; video footage of its operations would not reveal much more than a conventional warehousing system.

Integrating virtual components with physical ones: a value-creation matrix

It follows that managers need to develop organizations that have both virtual and tangible components. These components should fit together into a 'creative' organizational form that is in turn fit for its own purpose and able to achieve its goals. This is the challenge of the new decade for managers in complex economies. Orthodox management education and training would not have prepared managers for this task until recently. Even now, it is not self-evident how this mix would be put together, how it would work and whether it would ultimately create value.

There are thus two premises. First, 'going virtual' is a strategic option, the utility of which depends in part on the organization's capacity and needs and those of its customers and suppliers. Second, there is no single or unique virtual organizational strategy. Instead, each organization needs to search for a suitable mix of virtual and non-virtual components in order to achieve its ends. One must bear in mind that virtual organization is a means, not an end in itself. Adopting a virtual organization model will not solve all of a firm's problems; in some cases, it may raise as many barriers as it breaks down. Before choosing a virtual organizational strategy, then, firms should have answered the following questions:

- What is the nature of firm's product/service? Is it a physical, tangible product, or is it invisible and knowledge-based? Here one has to be sure that the whole product is considered. Does Amazon sell books, or does it sell its information and knowledge system over the Internet? In fact, of course, it sells both.

- What is the relationship between the firm and its customers? Do customers need a high-contact relationship, and if so, can this be transferred to the Internet or telephone? UK banks, in switching to call centres, are finding that as the level of personal contact between customers and bank managers declines, so the relationship between them deteriorates.

- What is the relationship between the firm and its suppliers? This can also depend on the nature of the goods being supplied. Parts and components that require physical shipment and are sourced on a just-in-time basis are often sourced locally, even from the factory gate. Knowledge and information, on the other hand, are not location-contingent and can be sourced from anywhere. Getting the sourcing mix right is another aspect of the virtual–real continuum.

- What is the relationship between the organizational elements in the firm? How can this relationship be strengthened? The nature of the inter-dependence between people, teams, departments and so on needs to be examined carefully. Some situations lend themselves easily to virtual working; others do not.

- What kinds of work are done within the firm? Can this be changed to become more efficient? Again, this will vary between departments and teams. A concentrated production team, for example, may not be able to work well virtually and may require close proximity; sales teams, more typically, are scattered physically and work through virtual links.

- What is the relationship between management and employees? How can this too be strengthened? One of the most common problems facing organizations that adopt virtual modes is loss of control and motivation. The removal of the physical proximity of management must be counter-balanced with mechanisms that will ensure relationships remain tight.

Virtual vs real: the choice for value

It may be harder to value a virtual organization because of its strong reliance on knowledge capital (Warner and Witzel 2000; see also chapter 6). Only a tenth of a firm's investment may be in IT; the rest may be in knowledge and org-anizational capital, not necessarily recorded by conventional accounting as investment in the corporate accounts, as a recent study by Brynjolfson and colleagues at MIT has suggested, based on 146 companies (see *The Economist*, 18 November 2000:6). This can lead to problems for virtual organizations in capital markets. As the recent boom and bust of dotcoms shows, capital markets and investors often have very little idea of how to assess value or set expect-ations when dealing with virtual firms. These problems add significantly to the level of risks these firms face. New work on value-based management suggests that firms need to be wary of false investor expectations (Ryan and Trahan 2000; Weiss and Wieandt 2000). The security of the operation for partners or employees may be dependent on the risk-element (as for example in the failure early in 1999 of Boo.com).

Figure 9.1 The value-creation matrix

On each dimension below, firms need to plot their position along the continuum. The sum of all these choices makes up the value-creation matrix.

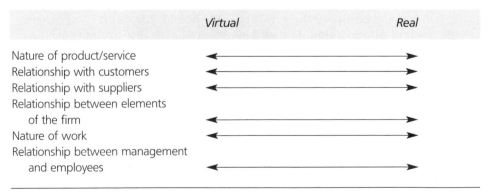

	Virtual	Real
Nature of product/service	◄──────────────►	
Relationship with customers	◄──────────────►	
Relationship with suppliers	◄──────────────►	
Relationship between elements of the firm	◄──────────────►	
Nature of work	◄──────────────►	
Relationship between management and employees	◄──────────────►	

The integration of virtual components with tangible ones must always be made with the idea that value creation will be the end result; further, of all the options available, the mix chosen should be the one that creates the maximum value for customers and shareholders. A dogmatic approach which says that 'virtual is best' may result in a system that does not deliver so well as a more hybrid mix – or, in some circumstances, even a conventional system.

It is for this reason that so many retailers have now adopted a twin-track strategy. While Amazon remains a virtual bookseller, its similarly US-owned rival Barnes and Noble now sells both online and through conventional retail outlets. It satisfies the needs of customers who like to buy online and those who like to browse in bookshops. Barnes and Noble is also more profitable than Amazon. In the UK, supermarkets such as Tesco have set up online shopping systems so that customers can buy food from home and have it delivered to the door. Only a small percentage of households in the UK buy their food in this way, and are ever likely to. But Tesco has succeeded in selling to that group that does buy online without compromising its position with respect to its more traditional customers. It is adding value in both markets.

Virtual vs real: the choice for co-ordination

The advantages of virtual co-ordination mechanisms are obvious. Telecommunications, the Internet, broadband and so on have the advantage of putting people in touch with each other instantly, no matter where they are in the world. Tele-conferencing, videophones and other types of technology means it is possible to not only hear but also to see the people you are dealing with. Even when people are working in near proximity, many of these forms of technology have the potential to speed up communications and save time. It is, for example, often faster and easier to e-mail a work colleague than it is to walk down the corridor to see them in person.

Virtual co-ordination reduces the time and costs that are required for co-ordination and thus improves efficiency. It requires an investment in technology, and also in training: those employees using virtual co-ordination systems need to be familiar with them, they need to be able to manage the technology itself and they also need to become experienced and comfortable at meeting and decision-making in virtual environments.

Virtual co-ordination systems are now very widely used, but they have never entirely become a substitute for face-to-face contact. Teams working in virtual contact may still schedule regular, if infrequent, contact meetings. Although virtual communication has become very sophisticated, it still tends to miss out certain nuances; even visual systems such as tele-conferencing, for example, are less good at communicating body language than face-to-face contact. And, too, virtual co-ordination systems are largely used for formal work and meetings; there is less informal contact such as private messaging, socializing and so on that help to build and reinforce corporate culture – indeed, some firms actively discourage the use of company systems for private messages.

In general, virtual co-ordination systems represent good value and are becoming widely used. But when setting up the value-creation matrix, managers need to know the limits of virtual co-ordination and when it will be necessary to use conventional face-to-face contact.

Virtual vs real: the choice for efficiency

Among virtual organization's many attractions is the belief that it brings both cost savings, particularly in the form of reduced infrastructure, and greater efficiency, especially in terms of knowledge management. However, there are limits to both these gains. Cost savings must be offset by increased investment in 'virtual infrastructure', especially communications technology. Recent reports have suggested that higher-performing organizations are more centralized than weaker ones – in other words, higher-performing firms had more people at head office. This may be due to the new information technology allowing a greater dilution of the spatial dimension with 'virtuality' leading to fewer people in the field, for instance. Productivity may be thus enhanced. But efficiency gains will only be realized if the organization's resources are correctly aligned with its new form. The key, as Miles and Snow (1978) pointed out some time ago, is that the organization should be fit for its purpose, not that it should follow some generically determined 'best' organizational form.

When determining the most efficient mix of tangible and virtual systems, therefore, it is necessary to look at the concept of efficiency on two levels. It is not sufficient to design each process in the most efficient way possible; it is also necessary that each process should contribute to organizational efficiency as a whole. At times it may even be necessary to allow some processes to become deliberately inefficient, at least when measured against standard benchmarks, in order to create more customer satisfaction, for example, and thus increase efficiency and productivity across the organization (Witzel 2003). This is particularly common in service organizations (Bateson 1995).

Virtual vs real: the choice for innovation

Traditionally, R&D facilities have been the main source of innovation, and these have tended to be concentrated in one location; global corporations like IBM might locate several research centres around the world to feed local subsidiaries, but this sort of investment is possible only for companies with very deep pockets. Virtual communication and co-ordination systems make knowledge-sharing over distances much easier and cheaper. Universities and defence-research consortia were already developing research projects of this type in the 1970s, enabled by the first ancestors of the Internet, and by the 1990s firms and groups of firms in many sectors had begun to learn from this experience.

Innovation now no longer needs to be concentrated in one place. Research, development and design teams can be set up with members working out of different offices or even from home, but all contributing to a project in some way. And, as Nonaka and Takeuchi (1995) insightfully point out, it is no longer necessary for innovation to come from dedicated, full-time research staff. Flexible teams can be put together from anywhere in an organization, dedicated to a single project, and disbanded when that project is complete. Virtual working facilitates this kind of team formation and working and makes it easy and efficient.

Again, though, there may be limits to what virtual working can achieve. Even in the examples cited by Nonaka and Takeuchi, there are occasions when it seems that innovation comes out of the synergy of people working, living and socializing in fairly close proximity to each other. These people tend to share mental models more easily, and adopt each other's ways of thinking more readily. One possible conclusion is that it may be that while explicit information is easier and cheaper to transmit virtually, the exchange of tacit information is more suited to tangible environments. More research is required on this, but for the moment, managers need to be aware of this possible limitation. Again, a mix of virtual and tangible systems according to the organization's own culture and needs will be required.

Virtual vs real: the choice for motivation

Virtual organization also brings with it substantial problems for HRM. People are easier to manage and motivate within fairly close geographical and cultural boundaries. Culture, as we have noted, is national and local, and HR are best located at this latter end of the spectrum. As many firms have found to their cost, global HR policies are seldom wholly successful. Managing such resources may need to be anchored here; in other words, 'think global, act local' may need to be a key plank of HRM (see Ng and Warner 1999). In theory terms, what is human may co-exist with what is virtual, but often may conflict with it. Human beings, namely employees, may prefer the tangible; they may want to relate to a local site, for example, say their call centre and the region in which it is located. They may relate less well to each other if in only virtual contact; a similar problem may exist relating to customers. Video-telephony may help here; video-conferencing has already been in existence for some years now and has been used for motivational purposes.

Distance cannot be entirely overcome by communications technology; personal contact and presence are required to at least some extent. (Even the virtual marketplace eLance.com has a physical headquarters, and clients often come to visit for the chance 'to see where it all happens'.) Paradoxically, this problem can be greater in industries that rely heavily on personal networks and contacts (shipbroking is a good example). There is also a view that loss of direct human contact can lead to less flexibility of response and more reliance on standardized procedures; this can have an impact on innovation and creativity, and also on market performance in some cases. Extending virtual organization 'too far' thus has its dangers in terms of keeping people motivated and focused on a common goal.

Virtual vs real: the choice for networking with suppliers and customers

Great steps forward have been made in this area, in terms of both 'virtual supply chains' and 'virtual retailing' (the so-called 'e-commerce'). Virtual supply chains (see Schary and Skjøtt-Larsen 2001) can be seen to pay dividends not only in terms of lower transaction costs and greater efficiency but also in terms of greater flexibility – they can be reconfigured quickly to meet changing customer needs – and better feedback of information between members of the chain. Virtual retailing has been more problematic. Of the various e-commerce companies that emerged in the late 1990s and then crashed in 2000, the hardest hit were the consumer retail (business-to-consumer, or B2C) operations; B2B e-commerce firms fared better, possibly because the nature of their operations allowed them to plug into other companies supply chains more easily.

Several factors serve to place limits on how far consumer retailing ventures can go virtual. First, there are the needs and demands of customers. For nearly a century, marketing literature has noted that for many customers, shopping – at least for some kinds of goods and services – is as much a social experience as an economic one. Many people genuinely like shopping in retail outlets, and these do not receive the same kind of satisfaction when shopping online. Second, the nature of some products does not lend itself readily to online retailing, at least not to all customers. Some people will buy clothing over the Internet, just as many were happy to buy clothing by mail order in the era of US-based firms Montgomery Ward and Sears, but others prefer to feel the fabric and try garments on. Most people prefer to 'kick the tyres' and test drive a car before buying it. Marketing of fresh or perishable products virtually is particularly sensitive, and this leads to a third issue. In order to be truly effective, B2C e-commerce has to be able to deliver goods to consumers at a place and time convenient to them, and this in turn, for all but the most intangible products, requires heavy investment in (physical) distribution and delivery systems. Many e-commerce firms relied on the postal and existing commercial courier services to deliver goods post-transaction to customers, and many were badly let down; the result was customer dissatisfaction and retreat to conventional forms of retailing.

The mix of virtual and tangible systems for building and maintaining supplier and customer networks, then, depends on four things: the nature of the supplier, the needs of the customer, the nature of the products or services being sold or moved along the value chain, and the firm's own facilities and competencies. All four of these factors must be considered when designing these networks in order to create the most possible value.

Conclusion

The conclusion to this chapter is fairly simple. There is no such thing as a completely virtual organization. Nor, indeed, is there any such thing as a completely tangible organization. Every organization consists of a mix of virtual and tangible elements, with physical capital and labour complemented by varying levels of intangible capital. Physical and virtual systems exist in the same organization; often, indeed, they interpenetrate each other. It can be very difficult, looking a particular process or function, to decide whether it is using a tangible or a virtual system.

There are no either/or choices; real vs virtual is a false dichotomy. The 'choice' is not between the two extremes, but of the best mix of elements that will add value and will exploit both tangible and intangible capital to the full. These decisions must not be made dogmatically, in the belief that any one system will give the best results. Rather, the aim should be to construct hybrid systems that will give the best results in any given situation.

And, the choice is never a final one. Times change: the environment alters, customer needs change, new technologies open up new possibilities. The choice, then, should reflect the dynamic needs of any business system, and should enable that system to be rapidly reconfigured or even replaced (with new mixes of real and virtual elements) if new and better options open up. It is for this reason that we stress the importance of assessment (from the CALV acronym noted in the previous chapter). Continuous assessment and understanding of changing needs and opportunities is required if the maximum value is to be created.

Case Study *Oticon*

Oticon is a Danish manufacturer of hearing aids that, in 1988, was moribund and being driven out of the market by larger competitors such as Siemens and Philips. Incoming CEO Lars Kolind realized that a revolutionary approach would be required, and responded with a total restructuring which he refers to as 'disorganization'. Today, organization at Oticon is a fluid affair with no departments or divisions: instead, project teams form and reform as they are needed. Project leaders (basically, anyone with a compelling idea) compete to attract the resources and people to deliver results. Project owners (members of the company's 10-person management team) provide advice and support, but make few actual decisions. The company has a hundred or so projects at any one time, and most people work on several projects at once.

Oticon has not abandoned physical space completely. It still uses its headquarters building near Copenhagen, where about 150 staff are based. However, within the building there are few formal offices, merely work stations with networked computers. Even these are often deserted as staff are frequently on the move around the building. Oticon's culture continues to value face-to-face contact, but does not restrict the sort of space where that contact can be. And for those staff members out of direct contact, telephone and e-mail systems enable them to continue to participate in the activities of their teams. The environment stresses motion and activity, rather than sitting at desks waiting for something to happen.

▶

Oticon runs an almost paperless office, and what little paper does come through the building is usually shredded and recycled at the end of the day. E-mail and mobile phones are much more important, especially for customer contact. Another important element of the Oticon culture is the think tank, a conference room where teams can meet and use various technology systems such as groupware systems and video-conferencing equipment for problem-solving and brainstorming.

Oticon has chosen an organizational model which reflects its own needs and own culture, and a mix of virtual and tangible organizational components which allows maximal use of knowledge capital and human capital, while at the same time increasing efficiency. Over the first four years of the new organization, Oticon doubled its size and its operating profits increased by almost 1000 per cent.

Source: 'This Organization is Dis-Organization', *The Fast Manager* (2002), www.fastcompany.com/online/03/oticon.htlm

10 | Managing the virtual organization: operations, motivation and co-ordination

Introduction

The previous chapter discussed virtual organization as being, in practice, a mix of tangible and virtual components, capital and systems. Managing in such organizations, therefore, requires a similar mix of 'traditional' management skills and 'new' skills. We discussed this mix of skills in chapter 8, and suggested that managing in virtual organizations is to be seen as an extension of general management. General management and virtual management have much common ground, including especially their common requirement for large amounts of intangible capital. We also suggested that, in virtual organizations, managerial responsibility is more devolved; each individual in a virtual organization takes at least some managerial responsibility for his or her own work. With a greater proportion of the organization involved in managerial work, the need for management tasks to be carried out efficiently and effectively is correspondingly greater.

We ended chapter 8 with a description of the four new sets of tasks required for managing virtually: communication, assessment, learning and valuation (CALV). Let us return to these for a moment:

- Communication: ensuring that knowledge flows are efficient and timely, linking all the elements of the organization to each other and to suppliers and customers.
- Assessment: the matching of the organization's goals with its form and structure on a dynamic basis, and altering or amending that structure when opportunities arise.
- Learning: the constant replenishment of an organization's stock of knowledge capital through such activities as training and education, R&D, environmental scanning and so on.
- Valuation: the continuous and dynamic reassessment of knowledge assets in terms of their present and future value to the firm.

The importance of these to the virtual organization has been demonstrated in parts I and II of this book. We have shown how communication is necessary to ensure that knowledge, the lifeblood of the organization, continues to circulate. Assessment is necessary to ensure that form and structure continue to match goals and customer needs; the need here is for structure to follow strategy, and technology to follow structure. Organizational form must not be driven by dogma, or by a perception that one form of technology or organization is inherently 'good'. Learning, as the first stage of the knowledge transformation process, creates the stocks of knowledge from which the virtual organization creates value; valuation creates the measures by which intangible capital is assessed.

All four of these new tasks are of critical importance. The exact nature of each, especially valuation, is currently in a state of some change and development as we continue to learn more about virtual management and virtual working. But, critical as they are, they are not the sole requirements for managing in virtual organizations. All the old tasks, which we identified in chapter 8 using the system developed by Henri Fayol – long ago, in France – and identified by the acronym POSDCORB, still remain essential. As the events of the past two years have graphically demonstrated, the information age may have transformed the business environment in many ways, but the old constraints of fiscal responsibility and the market, the old needs for accountability and good governance, people management and sound investment in technology remain powerful and firms ignore these at their peril.

It is the adaptation of these to a virtual environment that provides some of the toughest challenges for a manager in a virtual organization. Previous concepts of 'how to manage' have to be adapted, sometimes largely, or even replaced by new concepts. This chapter goes on to look at this issue in more detail, considering each of the seven 'traditional' tasks in turn. It poses a series of questions which managers must ask – and answer – both during the transition to virtual organization (or at least, to an organization with a high proportion of virtual elements in its mix) and on an ongoing basis. The exact answer to each question will depend on the organization itself and all the various cultural, environmental, organizational and other factors that render each business unique. The answers will vary from case to case, the questions will always remain the same:

- Who plans in virtual organizations?
- What are the costs and complexities of organizing virtually?
- How do people work in virtual organizations, and how are they rewarded?
- Who takes responsibility in virtual organizations?
- Who co-ordinates virtual organizations?
- Who reports to whom in virtual organizations, and where does the information go?
- How are assets valued in virtual organizations?

The impact of virtuality on planning: who does it?

Planning in conventional organizations is usually a central function (see Fayol 1917). Information may be gathered from many different sources, but the actual process of planning takes place very close to the organizational core, with primary responsibility lying with senior managers and directors. In a virtual web or other networked organization, the core is much smaller, and in some models is even non-existent; the question then arises as to who does planning and who takes responsibility for it. Also, given that virtual organizations tend to have fuzzy boundaries (Turksen 2000), there arises a further question of what entity is actually being planned for.

Both of the above issues are capable of resolution. Many planning models, not just those connected with virtual organizations, argue for more people to be included in the planning process, and a system whereby 'everybody plans' may at first sight seem ideally suited to a virtual web organization (see Franke 2002). However, practical problems quickly emerge, especially if not all members of the network have the same level of skill, or worse, access to the same levels of knowledge. Great care must be taken that members involved in the planning process have access to identical knowledge. Even so, other problems may arise. One of the most common is 'groupthink', whereby the members of the web adopt a compromise planning solution that may not necessarily be the best option.

The boundaries issue is more difficult, especially as members of a virtual organization – even more, a virtual web – will often be involved in other activities outside the organization. Membership of the virtual web may not be the only, or even the main, priority. Plans developed for the web organization may conflict with members' own plans and interests. Reconciling these will not be easy; it will be tempting for the more powerful members of the web organization to use their power to get their own way and push their own goals to the head of the planning process.

Both problems can be dealt with by establishing clear planning responsibilities from the outset, and by ensuring that one or more parties takes clear formal responsibility for ensuring that planning is done and to a satisfactory level. Such responsibility should be designed into the organization, not simply allowed to evolve.

The impact of virtuality on organizing: what restructuring is needed and what will it cost?

Many of the comments made about planning apply to the principles of organizing. In fuzzy teams members may not have clearly defined roles and may not fit into an organizational hierarchy. Nevertheless, this does not mean that anarchy can ensue. Organizing in the virtual world requires above all a clear focus on the goal (see Witzel 2000); indeed, the goal may be the only thing that is clearly visible in an otherwise unfocused world. We are not suggesting that a return to old-fashioned hierarchy is necessary, but we do argue that in any organization, all members must have a clear view of the organization's purpose and their own role in it. Duties and responsibilities need to be made clear, even if only in outline form, when the organization is first designed and established.

Much attention is paid in the literature to the role of the network broker or network hub (other names such as network manager or even what we may call the 'net-preneur' are also used). Establishing a clear central point of reference within the network can be very valuable in ensuring that information and knowledge flow freely and are accessible to all parties. Great care must be taken, however, that this network broker does not become a gatekeeper or controller, restricting rather than facilitating the flow of knowledge. For, as we saw above, a virtual organization without knowledge flows is literally a 'dead' organism. In the burst of enthusiasm for new web businesses, no small number were set up with hasty expectations and later left defunct.

When organizing virtually, it is important, too, to consider cost factors. Virtual organization is – or should be – a cheaper form of organization in that it reduces transaction costs and speeds knowledge flows etc. But it is not free: there are costs in terms of training and technology maintenance that have to be considered. And establishing a virtual organizational framework in the first place can be a highly expensive operation. During the late 1990s, many corporations sank large capital sums into technology investment; many of those firms are still waiting for that investment to be repaid. Once again, we repeat the mantra that structure follows strategy, and technology follows structure. Organizing in virtual space is, at the most basic level, just like organizing anywhere else: it aims to create an organization that can meet the firm's goals, and adapt that organization when the goals change, as they inevitably do. Clear focus on the needs of the virtual organization is a constant.

The impact of virtuality on staffing: how will people work and be rewarded?

Not everyone can work in a virtual organization but many young graduates and even non-graduates are finding themselves drawn into this new world of work, as traditional forms of employment shrink. Only some people have the skills to do so, and only some people are temperamentally suited for doing so. Humans are social animals, and many otherwise skilled people find themselves becoming demotivated and unable to work to full effectiveness unless they receive stimulation and recognition from colleagues and managers, and indeed customers and other stakeholders, in a face-to-face environment (see Bussing 2001). Not everyone who sells books successfully over a counter can do so over the Internet; sets of personal selling skills may require physical proximity to the customer. Internet selling often involves 'de-skilling' (see Braverman 1974), as is the case today in call centres.

Companies switching to virtual modes of operation have two choices: they can recruit staff who have the skills and temperament required to work virtually, or they can attempt to retrain existing staff. The first option brings up issues of selection: how will the firm identify the relevant skills and temperament in potential employees? What tools and knowledge will need to be acquired to do so? The second is a training issue. Along with the relatively straightforward matter of skills provision, there is the question of changing temperament through encouragement, motivation and support. How can the lack of physical contact be compensated for? Periodic physical visits or meetings, regular personal contact by telephone or over the Internet, mentoring systems, even 'e-discussion groups' and bulletin boards for members of staff and management to exchange views are all possible solutions.

The impact of virtuality on directing: where does the 'buck' stop?

The problems of directing or controlling a virtual organization are probably the most difficult and enduring. Virtual organizations, by their very nature, devolve large amounts of responsibility to individuals, teams and groups; they appear at least *prima facie* to be relatively less hierarchical and more 'democratic' than conventional businesses. While one should not exaggerate the degree of egalitarianism here, this feature is potentially a positive asset, as people are encouraged by the trust shown in them and the responsibility they are given. Most will do more than just maximize utility, that is they will go beyond the strict confines of doing the job for its rewards (salary, perks) to them individually and will seek to maximize benefits for the firm as well.

Problems tend to arise when the firm can no longer inspire employees to act creatively on its behalf. Proximate causes can include the breakdown of trust between employer and employee, systems failures, negligence, perceived lack of success in meeting personal organizational goals, or even entropy: the creeping boredom of doing the same job over a long period of time can be just as crippling in virtual work as in assembly-line production or a conventional clerical workplace.

When this happens, 'democratic' virtual organizations can be beset with the same kinds of problems that develop in democratic political systems, including factionalism and opting out. In factionalism, members of the organization in effect 'take sides', and begin putting the interests of their own group first; they may even seek to actively hinder the efforts of rival factions. Needless to say, although an element of creative tension can at times be useful, over the long run this acts to the detriment of the organization. In opting out, employees cease to identify with the organization's goals and begin putting in less effort; they may also choose to leave the organization and go elsewhere.

Both these problems, factionalism and opting out, occur in conventional organizations as well, but their effect on a virtual organization is more severe. As members divert more of their efforts into internal conflicts or external activities, the impact on the flow of knowledge will be noticeable. In both cases, members may deliberately withhold knowledge from the system, either for political gain or because they no longer care enough to participate. If this happens, then again, the knowledge management system can dry up and the virtual organization ceases to live. We must make it clear here that this is largely a question of degree and we would not want to labour the point unduly.

The impact of virtuality on co-ordinating: who paints 'the big picture'?

That co-ordination is more difficult over distance is a well-known axiom of military science, and it applies equally in management. Communications technology has been able to solve many of the problems of co-ordination over distance, but not all of them. Systems failures are the most common cause of co-ordination failure, and these can be both human and technical. A historical example once again makes the point. In 1939, RAF fighter squadrons operating in northern France were supplied with the wrong crystals for their radios, meaning that above an altitude of 7000 feet pilots could not hear their own controllers at base (they could, however, receive dance-music programmes on BBC radio with great clarity) (Townsend 1971).

Systems for co-ordination over distance need to be robust and able to handle the unexpected. They must not be overdesigned – a common fault – as this then requires both greater levels of operator skill and greater cost and time loss should the system fail and need to be repaired. Rather than spending money on a single complex system, the firm should consider simple systems with redundant capacity which can be activated in a crisis. The RAF again provides another good example. During the Battle of Britain in July–September 1940, RAF Fighter Command managed an aerial battle spread over many thousands of square miles of air space, involving input from more than 15 radar stations, 20 airfields and 600 pilots. The co-ordination system involved multiple telephone lines feeding into several sector-command centres simultaneously, with sector controllers then issuing orders to the fighter squadrons in the air; the sector control centres used technology no more complex than wooden blocks on a map table. Each control centre was linked to the others, and if one was bombed and put out of action, the others could quickly fill in the gap (Townsend 1971).

Even more than systems, though, co-ordination requires skill and ability on the part of those doing the co-ordinating. As in planning and organizing above, co-ordination should be a specific responsibility assigned to a few members of the organization, otherwise 'if everybody does everything, then nobody does anything'. Those tasked with co-ordination should be good at organizing both knowledge and people; a good sense of spatial awareness would be an asset. It may be worthwhile for firms to train or recruit personnel whose sole function is attention to co-ordination issues.

The impact of virtuality on reporting: who reports to whom, and where does the information go?

Reporting is both part of the problem and part of the solution. In the recent past, reporting issues have been seen as a critical factor in the business failures of, for example, the London-based banking firm, Barings. Examination of events, however, shows that in most of these cases it is failure to report, or reporting of inaccurate information, that it is the essential problem. The answer would to be more and better quality reporting which would allow all essential knowledge to be received throughout the firm.

But reporting is not just about control. Reports contain knowledge, which as we have seen is essential to the functioning of a virtual organization; failures in reporting bear within them the seeds of organizational failure. It follows that virtual organizations must be transparent, and that knowledge must not only be allowed to circulate freely, but must even be compelled to do so. Reporting is essential to the larger knowledge transformation process.

Once reports have circulated knowledge, it is equally essential to see that knowledge is organized and stored in an accessible manner, ready for future use. Reporting thus needs to be tied into a larger knowledge management system.

The impact of virtuality on budgeting and finance: how are assets valued?

As we have discussed in detail (Warner and Witzel 1999; see also chapter 6), the adoption of virtual forms of organization brings it with a series of financial-management issues. Financial managers to some extent have a head start over the rest of the organization when it comes to virtual thinking, because (whether they realize it or not) they have long been used to working and thinking in virtual spheres. On the other hand, much of past financial management has been driven by the use and management of virtually transmitted and recorded information and data. There is a key difference between this and the new virtual, knowledge-based organization, as we will see below. Financial managers need to transform their own thinking if they are to keep pace with growth of virtual organizations. Since the costs of managing capital also need to be confronted, there is a need for a new look at how to 'downsize' their financial infrastructure.

Finance professionals need to become more knowledge-based, more adaptive and more innovative if they are to be effective in a virtual environment. To this end, training programmes must be designed to ensure that financial managers are up to date with not only IT developments but also the new organizational and HR practices which are associated with them. The latter practices are still evolving, and managers should be flexible in devising solutions to suit their specific organizational requirements and not adopt textbook templates.

Another problem in this area concerns regulation. Governments tend not to like the virtual world very much; they cannot control it and they cannot tax it. Firms operating in a virtual environment are likely to become increasingly under pressure from national and international agencies to make their operations more transparent: 'virtual yet visible' may well become the regulatory watchword. The firm's finance professionals are likely to have a key role to play in this regard, helping to ensure that virtual operations remain compliant; and this in a regulatory environment that is likely to undergo rapid change in the near future.

The problem of valuing knowledge as an asset has not yet been satisfactorily solved. It can be argued that the share price of a virtual company (not all Internet stocks are virtual companies, but the two have enough common features to be comparable here), is a reflection of the value of the knowledge that company has; in other words, its knowledge capital. But how does an investor make a return if that knowledge cannot be turned into profit? Many Internet companies have not made a profit; many never will. Knowledge is static; investing in knowledge alone is like investing in a pile of rocks. Human capital is required to make that knowledge active and at least potentially profitable.

Conclusion

The changeover to virtual organization brings with it issues of both adoption and adaption for managers. They must first adopt new sets of practices and acquire new skills to manage the tasks of communication, assessment, learning and valuation. At the same time, they have to adapt more traditional management tasks and practices to this new environment. Just as the choice of the mix of tangible and virtual elements in the organization reflects a series of trade-offs aimed at achieving maximum utility and value, so the practice of management in such organizations requires a similar series of trade-offs, based on a pragmatic understanding of what is required to manage efficiently.

We have said that this mix will tend to be unique to each organization. This does not mean that there is no such thing as best practice in virtual organizations, or that benchmarking is not possible. But we suggest that best practice and benchmarks, like everything else in the virtual environment, will constantly change and evolve. New methods of managing will emerge, have their day, and then become obsolete in the face of further developments. None of this will affect the fundamental principles of planning, organizing, managing goals and objectives, managing people and intangible capital and so on. The building blocks will remain the same; the patterns that are created will constantly change.

Managing in virtual organizations does not require that the managerial rule book should be thrown away. Instead, it requires that the rules be creatively adapted to the new situation. The bottom line still exists, but there are different ways of reaching it. Customers have the same needs, but there are new ways of fulfilling them. People still want to work – to have a job – but there are new ways in which they can work, if they wish to do so. And so it goes. Above all, the key principle of managing virtually is not to forget the fundamental reason why businesses, and managers, exist: to serve customers.

Case Study *Guinness*

If e-business makes the technical implementation of B2B systems simpler, it does nothing to ease other aspects. And when it comes to human factors, upon which the success of these projects often hinges, e-business can present a raft of problems.

Human issues and cultural change have come to the fore in an integrated business programme (IBG) at Guinness, the originally Dublin-based brewing division of the Diageo PLC, a multinational food and drinks group. Helping employees negotiate the impact of new electronic systems has required careful and innovative planning.

Guinness is spending £40 million over three years to integrate systems and processes worldwide. The project aims to provide consistent information across the organization, pulling together the various elements of the Guinness operation. The next phase is a B2B intranet, now under development. In the shape of an online catalogue, the intranet will eventually link units within the organization as well as other businesses in the supply chain, handling the purchase of everything from brewery spare parts to the ingredients for beers.

Integration, says Guinness, is the name of the game; but integration can come in different shapes and sizes. Managers might have been tempted to take the easy path; and in effect replicate old business processes with new technology. As one senior manager commented, 'Not recreating old structures is many degrees more complex. It goes much deeper. You end up replacing old systems with a "new" company. Cultural change is at the heart of this kind of consolidation.'

For example, the IBP has led Guinness to integrate what were previously country-specific operations into a global frame. This involved various complex changes to employees' roles. The individual who used to order supplies for a single plant now has to consider the multi-plant perspective as well as the fact that, because figures entered are immediately carried across the supply chain, the system is more sensitive to quantitative errors.

As well as the big picture, there are numerous small-scale impacts to consider. To deal with the impacts, Guinness has consulted with staff about everything from new office layouts to car park places. Attention to detail has been reflected in implementation methodology. The effort is paying off; procurement savings so far stand at 9 per cent. But this is due not only to the investment in technology, but also to the investment in training people to use the technology to best advantage.

Source: *Financial Times*, 'FT-IT Review', 1 March 2000, p.12.

The virtual general manager

In this chapter we attempt to sum up our reflections on virtual management in general and what we have dubbed the 'virtual general manager' in particular (see Warner and Witzel 1999). We explore the characteristics of the virtual general manager and later go on expand upon how such managers can be trained and developed. We believe the virtual general manager to be a useful concept-ualization of a new and probably increasingly common phenomenon in the coming years.

Thus far we have spoken about virtual management and virtual organizations. We have not said much about the kind of manager that this type of manage-ment and organization require. Is the virtual general manager a completely new breed of manager, requiring revolutionary training and development programmes to create? Will the virtual general manager make the 'ordinary' manager obsolete? Or is the virtual general manager, like the virtual organi-zation, a concept that builds on existing types of management, adding on the new skills required for managing more effectively in virtual environments but still anchored in the fundamentals of management?

We use the term 'virtual general manager', not simply 'virtual manager', in order to make an important point. As discussed in chapters 8 and 10, we believe that virtual management and general management have close affinities. Managing in virtual organizations requires many of the same mindsets and attitudes that general management does, and many of the same skills. Virtual organizations require new managerial skills, but they do not render redundant any of the old ones. This is not to say that functional management is entirely dead, but the fuzzy, diffused and dispersed nature of virtual organizations puts a premium on a general approach to management. And so, if management in virtual organi-zations is effectively an evolution from general management, then it follows that the managers of those organizations also need to be virtual general managers.

Defining the virtual general manager

We define virtual general manager, therefore, as a manager in a virtual organ-ization who is responsible for managing across disciplinary boundaries and co-ordinating a variety of tasks and functions to reach a goal. Whereas in conventional organizations such managers are only usually found at the very top of the organizational hierarchy, in virtual organizations they form a large proportion – often the majority – of the overall management team. Specialists in areas such as IT and finance may be required to support them, but the main burdens of planning, organization, goal-setting and then managing the organization to reach those goals falls on the virtual general managers.

Virtual general managers may be found in relatively junior positions. The whole issue of senior and junior management levels itself can become problematic in virtual organizations, which tend to have fewer layers of hierarchy, and in which tasks and positions are more flexible. Even in those virtual organizations that maintain large head offices, virtual working tends to promote a more fluid structure and less dependence on hierarchy. However, it is fair to say that managers in virtual organizations tend to assume positions with general responsibilities – not just to carry out one function or task – earlier in their careers than do managers in more conventional organizations.

Managerial responsibility in virtual organizations tends to get pushed further down through the organization. As we have noted in previous chapters, employees who work virtually are required to take more responsibility for their own work, for issues such as project planning, quality control and so on. Employees who work virtually have goals set for them – a process in which they should ideally participate themselves – but are often left to devise their own best methods for meeting those goals. This means that much functional responsibility devolves onto the individual employees, leaving higher levels of management to concentrate on the 'big picture' of general management.

At the same time, virtual general managers tend to have fewer subordinates. This is especially true of those managers working in the field, away from head office. Often subordinates are limited to a few support staff such as IT or secretarial staff, and even these may be shared among more than one manager. General management is dependent on intangible rather than tangible capital, and the latter does not always require high levels of HR. Even at head office, some companies prefer to have large numbers of staff but these tend to be organized into teams rather than hierarchical departments. It could even be said that, while formal hierarchies tend to multiply subordinates after the manner of a bureaucracy, virtual organizations tend to multiply equals. A company converting to a virtual form might find it needs nearly as many managers as before to maintain its stocks of human capital, but those managers will be much more nearly equivalent to each other in terms of level within the organization, and will largely share a broad, general outlook and approach to management rather than being divided into isolated functional departments. If this can be achieved, then it is easy to configure and reconfigure project teams after the fashion described by Nonaka and Takeuchi (1995).

Virtual managers and general managers

Much of the above is not entirely new, even in the sphere of more conventional organizations. As we noted in part II of this book, the idea of intangible capital and of a knowledge dimension to work has been around for a couple of centuries. Therefore, it could be said that there has been a virtual dimension to management, especially general management, for a very long time.

But this is a long way from saying that all general management is virtual management. Conventional organizations tend to use general managers only at the upper levels of the organizational structure; virtual organizations tend to use them at nearly every level. General managers in virtual organizations are a small proportion of the whole management team; in virtual organizations, they may form a majority. General management in conventional organizations is characterized by continuity in terms of strategy, policy and management team composition; in virtual organizations, discontinuity and flexibility are the order of the day.

Many writers over the past two decades have urged conventional organizations to take on more flexible forms, and to make their managers into generalists (notably Peters and Waterman 1982; Kanter 1983; Peters 1987). The virtual organization has succeeded in doing this, not by changing the nature of management, but by changing the nature of organization and then evolving a new style of management to suit it. Is this move an 'evolution' or a 'revolution'? Possibly it partakes of a little of both; there is little doubt in our minds that virtual general management builds on and partakes of the core strengths of general management, but at the same time a revolutionary new outlook is required on the part of managers. These have to be prepared to conceive of themselves as virtual managers, and to be prepared to work and manage in the flexible and increasingly boundaryless environment of the virtual firm. The first big hurdle to virtual working is a psychological one, and only once that has been crossed can virtual working become a reality. Like so much else about virtual general management, the boundary between it and conventional general management is a fuzzy one. In terms of tasks and processes carried out, there is no clear-cut delineation, and often the progression into virtual methods of working is a gradual one.

Perhaps the best way of distinguishing between the two approaches to management is to identify the key areas where they differ. The best way of doing this is to look again at the primary tasks of general management (chapter 8) and to see how these need to change or alter to accommodate management in virtual organizations. Through this exercise, we can identify five principal 'gaps' between conventional and virtual general management. These gaps can be described as the skills gap, the network gap, the knowledge management gap, the boundaries gap and the direction and co-ordination gap.

Virtual management gaps

- The skills gap. It is commonly assumed that management in virtual organizations requires an entirely new set of skills that will sweep the old set aside. We argue below rather that new skills need to complement existing skills. The major need in terms of new skills is in the area of knowledge management and relationship management; technical skills are of secondary importance, though important none the less. A new repertoire of general-management skills is needed for the virtual organization of today and tomorrow.

- The network gap. A virtual organization – and in particular a virtual web organization – is a network, and needs to be conceived of as such. Unlike traditional hierarchies, which are static, the network needs to be organic and flexible. This organic nature of the network needs to be built into its design; it cannot be assumed that it will evolve. A new approach to organization design is thus required.
- The knowledge management gap. Although knowledge is often discussed in management terms, it is seldom conceptualized as a discrete asset requiring specific management systems. In virtual organizations, this needs to change. Knowledge needs to be seen as the essential core asset of the organization, which must be managed and used to be effective. An organic view of the virtual organization should see it in terms of components being linked by knowledge flows, in much the same way that the bloodstream carries blood and its essential components to various parts of the body.
- The boundaries gap. The hierarchical view of the firm creates boundaries, which are often designed to exclude as much as to include. Virtual organizations tend to be much less exclusive, and their fuzzy boundaries serve to include many who would not be considered part of a traditional firm. Approaches to planning and reporting, especially, need to be more inclusive and less exclusive than previously.
- The direction and co-ordination gap. In terms of conventional organizations, the debate has tended to focus on the merits of top-down versus bottom-up control or co-ordination. Neither is really appropriate for virtual organizations which, being fuzzy and dispersed, tend not to have a top and bottom, or indeed other conventional dimensions. Network organizations tend to exercise control from the centre outwards. However, as we mentioned above, this kind of control can be restrictive if the central controllers begin to conceive of themselves as gatekeepers rather than facilitators and co-ordinators.

New tasks for virtual management

What does this mean for management? Effectively, it means that managers now have another strategic option, the virtual option. However, this option does not consist in merely going virtual. Choices in the post-modern world are never so simple. Instead, the virtual option requires a blending of virtual and tangible management. Moreover, that blend must be carefully mixed, so as to suit the nature, structure, culture and goals of the organization in question. To borrow a phrase from Laudon and Starbuck (2000), the knowledge intensity of the firm is a key factor in finding 'the right level of virtuality'.

To fill some of these gaps, we believe it is necessary to supplement the original POSDCORB model (see Fayol 1917; Warner and Witzel 1999). The emphasis here must be on the word 'supplement'. We are not suggesting an entirely new model of management, because we are not dealing with an entirely new organizational form; instead, as set out at length above, companies need to create organizational syntheses, using both virtual and non-virtual components. The management of the virtual components requires additional tasks, but the tasks in the original model remain as important as ever.

The four additional management tasks required, we believe, are communication, assessment, learning and valuation (CALV). We considered these in chapter 8, but now let us look again at them in a little more detail. A short summary of each now follows.

Communication

Laudon and Starbuck (2000) note that in what they describe as knowledge-intensive firms – that is those at the high-knowledge end of the spectrum, in terms of products, processes, or both – the office is one of the vital centres of the workplace, as it is here that knowledge and information are generated and exchanged. However, modern technology means that members of the office no longer need to be physically proximate; a variety of methods for distance working mean that the office can become a virtual construct, an agglomeration of micro-offices all linked by telecommunications.

The communication task involves ensuring that knowledge flows are efficient and timely, linking all the elements of the organization and its suppliers, customers and other stakeholders. Communication is about rendering the organization both efficient and transparent. By communicating, we exchange knowledge, improve the quality of action and decision, and reduce or remove uncertainty and risk. Communication should be seen as a core part of the management task in virtual organizations. The new technology has now dramatically reduced the transaction costs involved in intra-organizational communication (see Coase 1937; Williamson 1985).

Communications are important in closing the last four of the five gaps described above. Organizational networks are built upon and function through continued communications, and this is true too of networks that go beyond the firm's boundaries. Communication is also vital to knowledge management, and to ensuring continued direction and co-ordination.

Assessment

Assessment in this sense is the matching of the organization's goals with its form and structure on a dynamic basis, and altering or amending that structure when opportunities arise. Because the virtual organization is a flexible and dynamic organizational form, its capabilities must be constantly tested and matched against organizational goals (which, of course, may also be dynamic and evolving). This assessment is not solely a planning function, but should be part of all management functions, and the results of ongoing assessment should be circulated as part of the knowledge management system. In this way the organization can become more self-aware and more able to anticipate and meet change.

The main impact of assessment in terms of the above gaps is on direction and co-ordination: continuous assessment of the firm and its value-creating opportunities helps to make direction and co-ordination more flexible, more democratic and more adaptable to new situations and opportunities.

Learning

Learning involves the continual replenishment of an organization's stock of knowledge capital through training and education, R&D, environmental scanning and other activities. Learning is a primary element of knowledge management, as it involves the creation and acquisition of new knowledge that is added to that already circulating in the knowledge management system. Using the organic metaphor of organization, by which we mean an organization which is capable of growing and evolving in the same manner as a biological organism, rather than requiring to be built in a mechanistic way, learning can be seen as the process of adding fuel to the organization, stimulating it into further growth and creativity. Organizational learning is perhaps the new value added of our times.

Learning is critical to the skills gap. Only through continuous learning can companies – and managers – acquire the skills they need to manage in a virtual environment.

Valuation

Valuation is the continuous and dynamic reassessment of knowledge assets in terms of their present and future value to the firm. Like assessment, this process must be continuous and a part of every manager's task. The valuing of intangible assets is much more than just a process of accounting for them as part of the organizational bottom line. Potential value as well as present-day value needs to be known. It is probable that new valuation measures will need to be developed to meet this need.

Valuation is important in terms of the skills gap in that the ability to value intangible assets will have an indirect impact on other managerial skills. It is important, too, in the boundary gap, particularly where intangible assets may be held in common with partners or other organizations. Finally, it is important in the direction and co-ordination gap, as it is the understanding of where intangible present and future value lie that will help to determine the best way forward for the business.

Training and education for virtual general management

Understanding these gaps, developing new skills and abilities, and above all reconfiguring the management task are areas in which management education and training can play a major role. But building a kind of management education for virtual managers is a great challenge in its own right.

This need comes at a time when many are already questioning the relevance of at least some forms of management education. For example, Mintzberg (1989) has very effectively pointed out the flaws in current management training, arguing that many business schools are still trying to train administrators and not leaders, and that management education is too often superficial and too far removed from the realities of business. In terms of general management, we have argued (see Warner and Witzel 1999) that the solution may be to develop ways of 'growing' general managers over a long term, probably within the context of a single firm or group of firms. Practical experience, in quantity, can be seen as a very important aspect of such training. Here also, in a modern context, the model used by Japanese firms, and also some Chinese family businesses – both of which tend to groom managers within the organization, using on-the-job training and giving prospective managers solid practical experience on the shop floor before promoting them through the ranks – may have relevance (Chen 1995).

The case of training for virtual general management lends some weight to this view. Certainly, training and improvement of virtual general management will have to be a continuous and career-long process: the impacts of new technologies and other environmental shifts that are making continuous learning so important for all managers are magnified in the virtual organization. We argue that to train virtual general managers effectively, there are four key requirements leading from the general to the specific:

- a new and more philosophical approach to management education;
- new general-management courses;
- new specialist courses, such as those relating to e-business that are already taught in a number of business schools;
- more and better practical techniques and applications.

A new approach

The requirements of virtual organization would seem to bear out Mintzberg's stricture that management education needs to train fewer administrators and more leaders, or at least, more people who are capable of thinking about the organization and its goals in broad terms. As we have noted, virtual organization requires much of the responsibility for functional management to be pushed further down the line to employees at lower levels, leaving the manager free to concentrate on more general issues and the big picture.

This in turn requires a much less functional approach to management training and education, and the development instead of a more philosophical and holistic view of the subject. Management needs to be taught as management and not as a collection of functions: marketing, finance, operations, HRM etc. with little or no effort made to show how these interrelate. And more material from outside the sphere of conventional management needs to be brought in, from fields such as psychology, sociology, philosophy, history, ethics and so on, to broaden the managerial mind and give managers fresh tools for analysing problems and creating solutions.

General-management courses

More immediately, there is a need for general-management skills – both the traditional kind and the newer ones required for general management – to be taught to managers much sooner in their careers. We argue that general management could easily be a core subject for MBA programmes, and even undergraduate business programmes. Managers in virtual organizations need to see the big picture and adopt a broad approach much earlier in their careers than do their more conventional counterparts.

These general-management courses need to concentrate on the things that general managers do, and not be simply 'functional-plus' courses. One option for organization of such courses might be to develop them around the seven task sets of the POSDCORB model (planning, organizing, staffing, directing, co-ordinating, reporting, budgeting), plus the four new task sets of the CALV model (communications, assessment, learning, valuation). Doing this would allow some of these tasks to be discussed and learned about in a unitary form, rather than divided up among functions. For example, planning is usually taught under separate headings as marketing planning, strategic planning, materials planning and so on. We would argue that in virtual organizations, planning is planning is planning; managers will be involved in all of these and more types of planning on a weekly, maybe even a daily basis, and that it is better to teach the underlying principles and ideas of planning rather than trying to provide detailed tool-kits for each type of planning on a separate basis.

New specialist courses

New specialist courses are required as well. Business schools and other training bodies have made a start with courses on e-commerce, but other specialist courses are needed too. Network management, managing people virtually, personal communications, knowledge creation and more general knowledge management, and assessment/valuation are all areas where more specialist knowledge is needed by the virtual general manager. As time passes, many of these subjects may be subsumed into the core management curriculum; but such is not the case now, and the pressing need for these types of knowledge and skills suggests that specialist courses may be the best way forward for the moment.

More and better practical techniques and applications

Related to the above, there is a need for researchers to develop practical general-management techniques and applications that can be easily passed on to managers in the field. To take just one example – the one we feel to be most important – the ability to value easily intangible assets such as organizational capital, knowledge capital and human capital is an urgent requirement. Methods, even subjective methods, of valuation need to be developed and transmitted if managers are to accurately assess the value potential of their firms.

Teams in virtual general management

Team-working is one of the most visible features of management in virtual organization, and team-working skills are of great importance to the virtual general manager. Teams exist in other organizations too, but they tend to be qualitatively different. Even Nonaka and Takeuchi's (1995) concept of the hypertext organization suggests that teams tend to be formed for specific projects and then disbanded, and that team members will also have ordinary functional work to carry on while they are involved in teamwork at the same time.

Virtual teams have several key features:

- They can be, and often are, dispersed, with team members working in different sites around the country or around the world. With no physical contact, communications between them are maintained by technologies such as the Internet, broadband etc.

- They are flexible and can be easily reconfigured. There is no need to disband a team when its work is done; instead, it can be reoriented towards new tasks. New members can be added to complement the skills of the existing team; members whose skills are less urgent can be deployed elsewhere; but the team itself can carry on in new directions. Core teams can have much the same lifespan as the company itself.

- Team-working should not be an extra, but should be the basic structure of how managerial work is done. As noted, with much functional responsibility pushed down the line, managers are free to concentrate on broader issues, and the team is the ideal venue for these. There is no reason why a manager cannot be a member of two, three or more teams, contributing his or her knowledge to each; and indeed this often happens in virtual space. Indeed, the same person can be a member of different teams belonging to different organizations.

Creating and managing a team in virtual space is both similar to and different from creating any other type of team. The requirements for setting up a team in terms of complementarity of knowledge, compability of interests and ability of team members to work harmoniously together are the same; the issue is complicated, though, by the need to work in virtual space. Team members have to be self-motivated and self-directing individuals who can carry out part of their work in isolation. Virtual teams are in contact with each other only when the communications technology is turned on, and typically – especially where members belong to more than one team – there will be long periods where members are out of touch with the rest of the team. In an atmosphere of physical isolation, many people find it easy to be distracted by more apparently pressing concerns 'nearer to home'. Many people switching from an office environment to tele-working, for example, find it difficult to maintain motivation without the external stimulus provided by the presence of other team members.

There is therefore additional pressure to ensure that team members are communicating and are working together. Ensuring this is the job of the team's manager, the person in the organization to whom the team reports on a regular basis. Ideally the manager should also be a member of the team, where it is then possible to monitor events and communications personally. If she or he is not a team member, there is a responsibility to monitor the team on a regular basis, perhaps talking with individual members on a private basis, to ensure that all are pulling together and contributing value.

All these are aspects of team-building and team-working that are brought out and highlighted by the pressures of working in virtual organizations. However, we would argue that the lessons of working in virtual teams can also be brought back and applied to more conventional teams working in physical proximity. In particular, the use of and attitude to teams as a managerial concept in the virtual environment can be applied in more conventional organizations as well. Here again is an area where the boundary between virtual and conventional organization can become blurred.

Creating a virtual management culture

Our final point with regard to the virtual general manager is the need to create and sustain a virtual management culture. Put in the simplest possible terms, this means the creation of a culture in which all managers and workers are able to adjust to and become easily familiar with a virtual environment. Working in virtual space should not seem like a challenge: it should be easy and natural, even affording a sense of relief and freedom after the 'constraints' of the conventional office.

Virtual cultures can be built around very simple concepts. Hatim Tyabji, CEO of the American electronics firm VeriFone (see case study at the end of this chapter), anchors his company's culture in the concept of 'insensitivity to distance and time'. Work in VeriFone carries on 24 hours a day at various sites around the world, with projects literally 'following the sun', being handed on from one office at the close of the working day to another office in a different time zone whose day is just starting. The idea is a simple one to conceptualize. Other concepts on which to base virtual culture might include:

- no boundaries between the firm and its customers;
- everyone in the firm participates in innovation and creative processes;
- knowledge is the firm's most valuable asset;
- continuous learning equals continuous value-adding.

Like all corporate culture concepts, these are easy to devise but harder to implement. The usual rules of corporate culture-building apply: there is a need for champions to carry changes through, and a need to ensure that everyone in the organization buys into the new cultural values, and understands what these mean for them personally. Culture change is hard. It is important not to make it harder by getting rid of the old corporate culture entirely. Few corporate cultures are entirely unsuited to virtual environments; nearly all have some ongoing value. Rather than starting a new corporate culture from scratch, it may be easier and cheaper to adapt the existing culture and take it forward into the virtual environment. Firms that already have strong traditions in areas such as customer service, innovation, R&D and innovative working practices will find this change much easier to manage.

Creating a virtual culture is an important step for management because, as we have said from the outset, it is the human beings within the organization who make the virtual environment happen. It is their collective acts of imagination that create the virtual dimension; they are the custodians of knowledge, the lifeblood of the virtual organization, and it is through their agency primarily that knowledge is transformed into value. In order for them to be able to carry out these functions to full effect, they need to work in an environment that they feel enables, supports and encourages them to do so. Particularly given the lack of direct supervision, lack of formal hierarchy and devolved managerial responsibilities, it is important to create and sustain a culture that motivates employees without overworking them, and encourages them to participate in the networks and communications systems that hold the firm together. In the virtual firm, psychology plays as big a role as technology in enabling workers and managers alike to pull together in teams and work towards the firm's goals.

Conclusion

To sum up, the virtual general manager needs to have all the skills required of a conventional general manager, plus additional skills necessary to work effectively in virtual environments. He or she must be capable of motivating employees from remote locations, maintaining communications network, managing teams in virtual space and creating a sustainable culture which enables and encourages working in a virtual environment.

To create such virtual general managers, we need to look closely at the kinds of training and education managers are given. We argue that a reconfiguration of at least some aspects of management education is required, focusing more heavily both on general management as a philosophy and set of practices and on the provision of important new skills through specialist courses. Learning and knowledge are important to the virtual firm at nearly every level. They are equally important to the managers in those firms, who require constant stocks of new knowledge to update and improve their management abilities. If, as de Geus (1988) says, a company's only sustainable advantage may be its ability to learn, then it would seem equally that a virtual manager's only lasting route to development and success lies in continuous learning. Finally, let us stress once again that important though technology is, it is only the enabler of virtual space, not the creator. Psychological and cultural factors are, if anything, even more important in virtual organizations than in conventional ones. More than anything else, the good virtual general manager must be a great manager of people.

Case Study   *VeriFone*

VeriFone is a global maker and distributor of credit-card-authorization terminals. Based in Redwood City, California, the company has offices around the world and revenues of around US$300 million (as of 1996). Under the direction of CEO Hatim Tyabji, VeriFone became one of the world's first largely virtual businesses, with features including global reach, location independence, an electronic knowledge network and a twenty-four-hour, seven-day operation.

The adoption of this model and its successful implementation is largely due to Tyabji himself, who believes in the virtual organization and has led his staff through the change processes. That change has been twofold: the introduction of the technology to enable the network and the cultural change required to make it work.

Tyabji describes the company's fundamental ethos as being 'insensitivity to distance and time'.

> *You know, if you are operating by conventional means – phone or fax or whatever – you have to know where someone is to work with them. The way we operate, it doesn't make any difference where people are. I don't give a damn where they are, so long as they can access e-mail. We have also proven that there is no reason why VeriFone can't have a twenty-four-hour day. VeriFone does have a twenty-four-hour day – and without people getting so frazzled they can't function.*
>
> *We have software projects that basically follow the sun. Our facility in Bangalore, India is one of our centres of excellence for networking and communications. So Bangalore develops the communications code for new products. Of course, that code has to be tested, and that work is done in Dallas. It also has to be integrated into our overall systems code, and that work is often done in Hawaii, where many of our systems engineers are based …because our people are distributed around the world, everything works in parallel. Before they go to sleep, the boys in Bangalore upload code and ship it to, say, Dallas or Hawaii, let those guys work on it, and then start again the next morning in Bangalore. Allowing our projects to follow the sun is something that we have done consistently – and with devastating efficiency.*

But Tyabji is strongly critical of those who attribute VeriFone's success to its technology networks.

> *Much of the stuff that has been written focuses on the form – e-mail, information systems – and not on the substance. The true power of running a company, the true power of growing any enterprise, is 5 per cent technology and 95 per cent psychology. With all this technology, you run the risk of becoming a robot. Leadership is not robotics.*

▶

Leadership is human. Leadership is looking people in the eye, pumping the flesh, getting them excited, caring about their families.

It's so easy to worship technology or to blame technology for problems that are human in nature: 'Our e-mail system isn't good enough.' The e-mail system has nothing to do with anything. Companies have this funny idea – they forget that human beings are human beings. Not here. Nothing I say should be construed as pie-in-the-sky stuff that doesn't take into account the frailties of human nature. I'm extremely mindful of the frailties of human nature. What I do is acknowledge those frailties and address them, rather than pretend they don't exist.

'We expect people at VeriFone to go above and beyond the call of duty – not because they are forced to, but because they want to. The people who join this company change. Their pace of life changes. Their intensity changes. Their emotional level changes...We've got this naive belief that if you have a fundamental set of values, and if you treat people with dignity, by and large you attract the right people. By the way, more than half our people work outside the United States. And even within the United States, our people come from different backgrounds, different industries, different ethnic origins. We have a global, multifaceted population. But we approach recruiting – whether it's in San Francisco or Santiago, Chile – the same way everywhere.

Source: 'At Verifone It's a Dog's Life (And They Love It)', *The Fast Manager* 2001, www.fastcompany.com/online/01/vfone.html

12 Summing up

Any book such as this one runs the risk of raising more questions than it answers. In particular, readers will have noted that we have used two terms with seeming interchangeability: managing in virtual organizations, the title of the book, and virtual management. It can be said that these are – in theory at least – two different things: the former refers to the art of management in a specific type of organization, the latter to a specific set of management practices.

This point may be true, but in our view the two concepts overlap to the point of becoming conceptually almost indistinguishable. This short final chapter aims to present the reader with the last word on the matter. To explain, let us look at a few definitions that can be drawn from the material presented in the book so far.

- Virtual organization: an organization that uses communications technology to substitute for physical structure, enabling work to be dispersed and decentralized, the organization itself becoming more flexible and fuzzy in nature. Such organizations are by nature knowledge-intensive and heavily reliant on intangible capital. They also require employees to take on more personal managerial responsibilities.
- Virtual management: management that uses communications technologies to substitute for physical contact with the business units and people being managed. Instead of personal, individual oversight of employees, virtual management relies on co-ordination, motivation and the building of flexible, networked teams to achieve goals.
- Virtual manager: any manager working in a virtual environment. Virtual managers possess high levels of communications skills, are adept at managing knowledge and know how to value and employ intangible capital.

If the choice between virtual organization and conventional forms of organization was a simple choice between A or B, then it might follow that the choice between virtual/conventional management/managers was equally simple. A conventional organization, we might argue, is managed conventionally by old-style line managers; a virtual organization is managed virtually by virtual managers. But, as we have argued throughout this book, that choice presents a false dichotomy.

The virtual mix

All of our 'conventional' organizations have a virtual dimension, in which long-distance communication takes place – it does not matter whether that communication is by telegraph, telephone, e-mail, or satellite-linked virtual conferencing – and where knowledge circulates. Nonaka and Takeuchi (1995) urge managers to conceptualize their organizations as existing on several levels at once – some real, some virtual. Such a formulation does not require a switch to virtual organization in toto, it merely requires the recognition of a virtual dimension in organizational theory.

Similarly, even the most 'virtual' of organizations, from Reuters to Amazon.com, require some physical space in which to operate, even if that space is widely scattered. And virtual organizations require two other tangible components: technology – or, at least, hardware – to support and enable the virtual dimension, and people to create that dimension using their own knowledge and imagination.

All organizations, we have argued, consist of a mix of virtual and tangible elements. What we call conventional organizations have a higher proportion of tangible elements and a stronger reliance on tangible capital. What we call virtual organizations have a higher proportion of intangible elements and a stronger reliance on intangible capital in terms of economics. But there are many different positions that can be occupied along the continuum.

It follows, then, that management is in practice a mix of tasks and approaches to management. And finally, managers must have the skills to manage both tangible and virtual assets, to work in both the real and virtual worlds. There is no either/or choice for managers in today's economic environment. If they neglect either conventional, tangible management or virtual management, they run the risk of destroying value and hampering competitiveness.

When we speak, therefore, of managing in virtual organizations and virtual management, we are not talking about a single way of managing. We are talking about a vast variety of different combinations of skills and tasks and hybrid forms of organization; a rich variety of scenarios and mixes to choose from. If there can be said to be a single art to virtual management, it consists in knowing how to select the right mix of elements, to configure the organization in such a way as to best follow its strategy, and then to deploy the right combination of technology and people, tangible and intangible resources, to follow that goal. Such is the challenge that confronts the virtual manager, not only when setting up a virtual organization, but constantly throughout that organization's life.

Figure 12.1 The virtual continuum

Tangible . . . . Virtual

Who should go virtual?

Before we answer this question, there is another question that must be addressed. Surely by describing the virtual organization and virtual management in these terms we have cast the net too widely? By this definition, are not all organizations then virtual organizations, and all managers virtual managers? And if that is so, do not the concepts of virtual organization and virtual management become diffuse and lose their potency?

It is possible that the day will come when all, or nearly all, organizations are virtual organizations. What this means is not that every business will become solely an e-business, as was once envisioned in the 1990s, but rather that every business will seek to exploit and develop its virtual dimensions. This does not mean abandoning tangible business elements; indeed, the latter are a vitally important platform from which to launch into virtual space. But the importance of the virtual dimension will increase; the value of intangible capital will become more widely measured and recognized; and the manager of the future will spend more and more of his or her time working in virtual environments.

But all that lies in the future. At present, few businesses fully understand the potential of virtual space. Even some of those firms that call themselves 'virtual organizations' today are highly biased towards conventional forms, and their exploration of virtual space has been limited to a few business areas or activities. As discussed in chapter 11, what seems to be needed now is not so much a revolution in the way management is done, as in the way it is thought about. We know that the emphasis on intangible capital in virtual organizations as opposed to conventional organizations is a difference of degree rather than kind; the dependence on intangible capital is far stronger in the former, but is by no means negligible in the latter. In existing models of general management, we already have an adequate basis from which to begin building a model of virtual management.

What is most required now is a realistic way of thinking about and managing virtual organizations. First, virtual organization should not be approached as if it was a panacea, a solution to all business problems. Virtual organization has very real costs and very real challenges. Contrary to some assumptions, virtual organization is not simple; to be effective, it requires a degree of complexity beyond anything most managers have encountered. But, on the other hand, the potential advantages of virtual organization are also very great: lowering transaction costs within and between firms, greater flexibility, better ability to manage intangible capital and create value from it – these are all benefits that could be critical to continued competitive success.

As much as anything, managing in virtual organizations is a psychological issue. It requires, before anything else, an effort of human imagination and creativity, not only to develop virtual space in the first place but then to go on and manage and work within that space, and to continue to develop and expand it. The potential of virtual space is limited, we might argue, indeed by only two things: human imagination and knowledge on the one hand, and technological capacity on the other. And the first can usually be employed to expand the second, if such is required.

If we take 'going virtual' to mean not a wholesale conversion to a virtual form of organization in every aspect and every business function, but rather the selection of a mix of virtual and tangible elements which best fits the needs of the business and its customers, then there is no reason why all companies cannot explore the virtual option more fully. Moving into the virtual dimension allows the potential for more growth – at a cost, true, but with great potential for future value.

What are the implications of going virtual?

Creating a virtual organization – that is one with a high level of virtual components and a strong reliance on intangible capital – is not cost-free. A large amount of investment is required. Technology is needed to enable virtual space. Time and resources for planning are needed, to structure the organization correctly and to ensure that the technology investment fits with the organization's needs. Training is needed, both to use the new technology and to learn to think about and imagine the new virtual dimension. Training may be needed too for knowledge management and other related activities. Finally, there will be costs associated with the organizational transition itself, moving or relocating people, changing their terms of work and so on.

There is a risk, too, when going virtual, that even if the firm manages to successfully adapt its own organization, it may find that its customers, suppliers and other external stakeholders are not yet ready to join it in virtual space. A considerable amount of marketing needs to be done to explain to customers, in particular, why the change is taking place and what the benefits – and, if any, downsides – will be to them.

Finally, there are risks as far as capital markets are concerned. We have noted how in the wake of the dotcom crash, both debt and equity markets are evincing scepticism about virtual firms, e-commerce firms, and the whole of the high technology-based sectors. Until adequate measures are found for valuing intangible capital, these firms will have to be very careful to demonstrate tangible value. The risks of being undercapitalized are very high at the moment, and firms must be careful not to expand too far beyond the limits of their capital resources. Lenders, in particular, are not interested in funding intangible assets.

These are the risks and the downsides. For many firms these risks will be worth running. The positive aspects of virtual co-ordination have been stressed many times; let us be reminded of the key ones again:

- lower transaction costs;
- lower operating costs;
- greater flexibility;
- better management of knowledge;
- more value-creating opportunities.

Conclusion

The challenge of managing in virtual organizations is to achieve and sustain the right 'fit' between the people, technology and knowledge the organization possesses. To do this, managers must first ensure that they have determined their goals and set out a workable strategy to achieve them. They must then develop the right organizational structure with the best mix of real and virtual elements for meeting that goal. Finally, they must invest in the right technology to enable the requisite virtual space to be created.

These are not one-off decisions. Managing in virtual space means moving into a more flexible, fuzzy environment where change is rapid and new opportunities and challenges are constantly emerging. The mix, once established, needs constantly to be adjusted. Teams need to be reconfigured and redesigned to meet new tasks. Systems, too – whether managerial or technological – need constant updating and replacing. And a corporate culture that enables and supports all this activity needs to be maintained, upheld and reinforced.

Managing in virtual organizations is dynamic. Each challenge, once solved, is succeeded by another. Each goal, once met, is replaced by another. The task of management never ends. But for the manager who has the drive, the energy, the ability and the knowledge to keep pace with change – even to keep ahead of change and help to bring it about – the rewards will be very high. The age of the virtual organization did not end with the dotcoms; indeed, it has hardly begun. Virtual organization is a hard and challenging environment; it is also the way of the future.

Bibliography

Albert, S. and K. Bradley (1997) *Managing Knowledge: Experts, Agencies and Organizations*, Cambridge: Cambridge University Press.

Argyris, C. (1971) *Management and Organizational Development*, New York: McGraw-Hill.

— (1993) *On Organizational Learning*, Oxford: Blackwell.

Argyris, C. and D. Schön (1978) *Organizational Learning*, Reading, MA: Addison-Wesley.

Babbage, C. (1835) *The Economy of Machinery and Manufactures*, London: Charles Knight.

Barnard, C.I. (1938) *The Functions of the Executive*, Cambridge, MA: Harvard University Press.

Barnatt, C. (1995) 'Office Space, Cyberspace and Virtual Organization', *Journal of General Management* 20 (4), Summer: 78–92.

Bateson, J.E.G. (1995) *Managing Services Marketing*, Fort Worth, TX: Dryden.

Bernays, E.L. (1928) *Propaganda*, Port Washington, VT: Kennicat Press.

Bleeker, S.E. (1998) 'The Virtual Organisation', in G.R. Hickman (ed.), *Leading Organizations*, Thousand Oaks, CA: Sage.

Boisot, M. (1995) *Information Space: A Framework for Learning in Organizations, Institutions and Culture*, London: Routledge.

— (1998) *Knowledge Assets: Securing Competitive Advantage in the Information Economy*, Oxford: Oxford University Press.

Braverman, H. (1974) *Labor and Monopoly Capital: Degradation of Work in the Twentieth Century*, New York: Monthly Review Press.

Brech, E.F.L. (2002) *The Evolution of Modern Management*, Bristol: Thoemmes Press, 5 vols.

Breukel, A.W.V. (n.d.) 'The Decline of Efficiency in Management Thinking', draft article. We are grateful to Dr Breukel for showing us this work in progress.

Bridges, W. (1995) *Jobshift: How to Prosper in a Workplace Without Jobs*, New York: Perseus.

Bussing, A. (2001) 'Motivation and Satisfaction', in M. Warner (ed.), *International Encyclopedia of Business and Management*, London: Thomson Learning, 4585–4597.

Chandler, A.D. (1962) *Strategy and Structure: Chapters in the History of American Industrial Enterprise*, Cambridge, MA: MIT Press.

— (1977) *The Visible Hand: The Managerial Revolution in American Business*, Cambridge, MA: Harvard University Press.

Chen, M. (1995) *Asian Management Systems: Chinese, Japanese and Korean Styles of Business*, London: Routledge.

Clark, J.J. (2000) *The Tao of the West*, London: Routledge.

Coase, R.H. (1937) 'The Nature of the Firm', *Economica* 4 (16): 36–405.

Collins, J. and J. Porras (1994) *Built to Last*, New York: HarperBusiness.

Cummins, J.C. (2002) 'A New Approach to the Valuation of Intangible Capital', www.nber.org/~confer/2002/criw.htm

Daly, A. (2001) 'Human Capital', in M. Warner (ed.), *International Encyclopedia of Business and Management*, London: Thomson Learning, 2603–2609.

Danthine, J.P. (2002) 'Intangible Capital, Asset Pricing and Firm Value', www.fmpm.ch/docs/5th/jin_danthine.htm

Davenport, T. (1993) *Process Innovation*, Boston: Harvard Business School Press.

— (1998) *Working Knowledge*, Boston: Harvard Business School Press.

Davis, S. and C. Meyer (1998) *Blur: The Speed of Change in the Connected Economy*, Oxford: Capstone.

de Geus, A. (1988) 'Planning as Learning', *Harvard Business Review* 66 (2): 70–74.

Dell, M. (1999) *Direct from Dell: Strategies that Revolutionized an Industry*, New York: HarperBusiness.

Den Hertog, F. and T. Tolner (2001) 'Groups and Teams', in M. Warner (ed.), *International Encyclopedia of Business and Management*, London: Thomson Learning, 2429–2439.

Diebold, J. (1985) *Managing Information: The Challenge and the Opportunity*, New York: AMACOM.

Donkin, R. (2001) *Blood, Sweat and Tears*, London: Texere.

Drucker, P.F. (1954) *The Practice of Management*, London: Heinemann.

— (1967) *The Effective Executive*, London: Heinemann.

— (1974) *Management: Tasks, Responsibilities, Practices*, London: Heinemann.

— (1989) *The New Realities*, Oxford: Heinemann.

— (1995) *Managing in a Time of Great Change*, Oxford: Butterworth-Heinemann.

— (1999) 'Knowledge-Worker Productivity: The Biggest Challenge', *California Management Review* 41 (2): 79–94.

Dunbar, R. (2001) 'Virtual Organizing', in M. Warner (ed.), *International Encyclopedia of Business and Management*, London: Thomson Learning, 6709–6717.

Dzinkowski, R. (2002) 'Knowledge for All: Knowledge Sharing at the World Bank', *Financial Times Mastering Management Online*, June, www.ftmastering.com/mmo/

The Economist (2000) 'A Survey of E-Management', *The Economist*, 18 November: 1–52.

Edvinsson, L. (1997) *Intellectual Capital*, New York: HarperBusiness.

Emerson, H. (1913) *The Twelve Principles of Efficiency*, New York: The Engineering Magazine Co.

Engels, F. (1938) *Engels on Capital*, trans. L.E. Mins, London: Lawrence and Wishart.

Evans, P. and T. Wurster (2000) *Blown to Bits: How the New Economics of Information Transforms Strategy*, Boston: Harvard Business School Press.

Fayol, H. (1917) *General and Industrial Management*, trans I. Gray, New York: David S. Lake, 1984.

Fitton, R.S. (1989) *The Arkwrights: Spinners of Fortune*, Manchester: Manchester University Press.

Follett, M.P. (1937) 'The Process of Control', in Luther Gulick and Lyndall Urwick (eds), *Papers on the Science of Administration*, New York: Institute of Public Administration, Columbia University.

Ford, H. (1926) *Today and Tomorrow*, Garden City, NY: Doubleday.

Forrester, J.W. (1961) *Industrial Dynamics*, Portland, OR: Productivity Press.

Foucault, M. (1975) *Discipline and Punish*, trans. A. Sheridan, New York: Pantheon, 1977.

Franke, U. (1999) 'The Virtual Web as a New Entrepreneurial Approach to Network Organisations', *Entrepreneurship and Regional Development* 11: 203–209.

— (ed.) (2002) *Managing Virtual Web Organizations in the Twenty-first Century: Issues and Challenges*, Hershey, PA: Idea Group Publishing

Fruin, W.M. (1992) *The Japanese Enterprise System*, Oxford: Oxford University Press.

Goldman, S.L., R.N. Nagel and K. Preiss (1995) *Agile Competitors and Virtual Organisations*, New York: Van Nostrand Reinhold.

Graham, G. (1999) *The Internet: A Philosophical Inquiry*, London: Routledge.

Greenfield, S. (1997) 'The Brain as a Computer', lecture delivered at Gresham College, London, 27 November.

Grenier, R. and G. Metes (1995) *Going Virtual: Moving Your Organisation into the 21st Century*, Upper Saddle River, NJ: Prentice-Hall.

Hamilton, I.M.S. (1922) *The Soul and Body of an Army*, London: Edward Arnold.

Hammer, M. and J. Champy (1993) *Reengineering the Corporation*, London: Nicholas Brealey.

Handy, C. (1976) *Understanding Organizations*, London: Penguin.

— (1989) *The Age of Unreason*, London: Business Books.

— (1996) *Beyond Certainty*, London: Arrow.

Harcourt, G.C. (2001) 'Marx, Karl Heinrich', in M. Warner (ed.), *International Encyclopedia of Business and Management*, London: Thomson Learning, 4355–4362.

Heller, F. (2001) 'Leadership', in M. Warner (ed.), *International Encyclopedia of Business and Management*, London: Thomson Learning, 3786–3796.

Heller, F. and B. Wilpert (1979) 'Managerial Decision Making: An International Comparison', in George W. England, Anant R. Neghandi and Bernhard Wilpert (eds), *Organizational Functioning in a Cross-Cultural Perspective*, Ohio: Kent State University Press.

Hofstede, G. (1991) *Cultures and Organizations*, London: McGraw-Hill.

— (2001) 'Organizational Culture', in M. Warner (ed.), *International Encyclopedia of Business and Management*, London: Thomson Learning, 4936–4953.

Joynt, P. and M. Warner (2001) 'Technology Strategy, International', in M. Warner (ed.), *International Encyclopedia of Business and Management*, London: Thomson Learning, 6387–6396.

Kanter, R.M. (1983) *The Change Masters: Innovation for Productivity in the American Corporation*, New York: Simon & Schuster.

— (1988) *When Giants Learn to Dance*, New York: Simon & Schuster.

Keller, K.L. (1997) *Strategic Brand Management: Building, Measuring and Managing Brand Equity*, Englewood Cliffs, NJ: Prentice-Hall.

Khalil, E.L. (1996) 'Networks and Organizations', in M. Warner (ed.), *International Encyclopedia of Business and Management*, 1st edn, London: Thomson Learning, 3630–3635.

Kolmogorov, A. (1965) 'Three Approaches to the Definition of the Notion of Amount of Information', in A.N. Shiryayev (ed.), *Selected Works of A.N. Kolmogorov*, Vol. III: 188.

Kotter, J.P. (1986) *The General Managers*, New York: Macmillan.

— (1990) *A Force for Change: How Leadership Differs from Management*, New York: The Free Press.

Langlois, R.N. (1999) 'The Coevolution of Technology and Organisation in the Transition to the Factory System', in P.L. Robertson (ed.), *Authority and Control in Modern Industry*, London: Routledge: 36–55.

Laudon, K. and W.H. Starbuck (2000) 'Organizational Information and Knowledge', in M. Zeleny (ed.), *The IEBM Handbook of Information Technology in Business*, London: Thomson Learning: 218–229.

Lev, B. (2002) 'Intangible Capital Report', www.brook/edu/es/research/projects/intangibles/ic.htm

Li, F. (1995) *The Geography of Business Information*, Chichester: Wiley.

Loveridge, R. (2001) 'Technology and Organization', in M. Warner (ed.), *International Encyclopedia of Business and Management*, London: Thomson Learning, 6355–6368.

Marshall, A. (1890) *Principles of Economics*, London: Macmillan.

Marshall, A. and M.P. Marshall (1879) *The Economics of Industry*, London: Macmillan.

Marx, K. (1933) *Das Kapital*, London: J.M. Dent & Sons.

Maslow, A. (1954) *Motivation and Personality*, New York: Harper & Row.

McLuhan, M. (1962) *The Gutenberg Galaxy*, New York: McGraw-Hill.

Menendez-Olonso, E. (2002) 'How do Intangible Assets Affect Capital Decisions?', *Corporate Finance Review* (March–April): 17–24.

Miles, R.E. and C.C. Snow (1978) *Organizational Strategy, Structure and Process*, New York: McGraw-Hill.

Mintzberg, H. (1989) *Mintzberg on Management: Inside the Strange World of Organizations*, New York: The Free Press.

Morgan, G. (1986) *Images of Organization*, Newbury Park, CA: Sage.

— (1993) *Imaginization*, Thousand Oaks, CA: Sage.

Mumford, L. (1967) *The Myth of the Machine*, London: Secker & Warburg, 2 vols.

Ng, S-H., and M. Warner (1999) 'Human resource management in Asia', in B. Morton and P. Joynt (eds), *The Global HR Manager*, London: IPD.

Nolan, P. (2001), *China and the Global Business Revolution*, London: Palgrave.

Nonaka, I. and N. Takeuchi (1995) *The Knowledge-Creating Company*, Oxford: Oxford University Press.

O'Hara, M. and D.A. Peak (2000) 'Intellectual Property', in M. Zeleny (ed.), *The IEBM Handbook of Information Technology in Business*, London: Thomson Learning: 119–125.

Osborne, R. (2001) 'Entrepreneurial Strategies', in M. Warner (ed.), *International Encyclopedia of Business and Management*, London: Thomson Learning, 1759–1762.

Palmer, J.W. and C. Speier (1997) 'A Typology of Virtual Organizations: An Empirical Study', hsb.baylor.edu/ramsower/aic.ac.97/palm_spe.htm

Papows, J. (1999) *Enterprise.com*, London: Nicholas Brealey.

Parikh, J. (1991) *Managing Your Self*, Oxford: Blackwell.

Parsons, C.C. (1909) *Business Administration*, Chicago: A.W. Shaw.

Parsons, T. (1959) 'An Approach to the Sociology of Knowledge', in T. Parsons, *Sociological Theory and Modernist Knowledge*, New York: The Free Press, 1969.

Pennings, J. (2001) 'Innovation and Change', in M. Warner (ed.), *International Encyclopedia of Business and Management*, London: Thomson Learning, 3031–3048.

Penrose, E. (2001) 'Growth of the Firm and Networking', in M. Warner (ed.), *International Encyclopedia of Business and Management*, London: Thomson Learning, 2040–2048.

Peters, T.J. (1987) *Thriving on Chaos: Handbook for a Management Revolution*, New York: Knopf.

— (1991) *Beyond Hierarchy: Organizations in the 1990s*, New York: Knopf.

— (1992) *Liberation Management: Necessary Disorganization for the Nanosecond Nineties*, New York: Knopf.

Peters, T.J. and R.H. Waterman (1982) *In Search of Excellence: Lessons from America's Best-run Companies*, New York: Harper & Row.

Polanyi, M. (1958) *Personal Knowledge*, Chicago: University of Chicago Press.

Portanger, E. (2002) *Boo Hoo: A Dot.Com Story from Concept to Catastrophe*, London: Arrow.

Porter, M. (1980) *Competitive Strategy: Techniques for Analyzing Industries and Competitors*, New York: The Free Press.

Read, D. (1992) *The Power of News: A History of Reuters, 1899–1989*, Oxford: Oxford University Press.

Ryan, H. and E. Trahan (2000) 'Value-Based Management Systems', *Corporate Finance Review*, July–August: 3–13.

Schary, P.B. and T. Skjøtt-Larsen (2001) *Managing the Global Supply Chain*, Copenhagen: Copenhagen Business School Press.

Schumpeter, J. (1934) *The Theory of Economic Development*, trans. Redvers Opie, Cambridge, MA: Harvard University Press.

— (1954) *History of Economic Analysis*, ed. E. Boody Schumpeter. New York: Oxford University Press.

Semler, R. (1993) *Maverick! The Success Story Behind the World's Most Unusual Workplace*, London: Arrow.

Senge, P.M. (1990) *The Fifth Discipline*, New York: Century Business Books.

Senior, N. (1850) *Political Economy*, London.

Smith, A. (1776 [1976]) *An Inquiry into the Nature and Causes of the Wealth of Nations*, ed. R.H. Campbell and A.S. Skinner, Oxford: Oxford University Press.

Smith. C. (2001) 'Labour Process', in M. Warner (ed.), *International Encyclopedia of Business and Management*, London: Thomson Learning, 3734–3743.

Srinivasan, P. (2002) 'How Can Brand Equity Be Measured?', www.ifmr.com/new/eq.pdf

Stewart, T. (1997) *Intellectual Capital*, New York: Doubleday.

Strassman, P. (1990) *The Business Value of Computers*, New Canaan, CT: Information Economics Press.

Svelby, K.-E. (1997) *The New Organizational Wealth*, San Francisco: Barrett-Koehler.

Taylor, F.W. (1895) *A Piece-Rate System*, New York: American Society of Mechanical Engineers.

— (1911) *Principles of Scientific Management*, New York: W.W. Norton & Co.

Tomer, J. (1998) *The Human Firm*, London: Routledge.

Townsend, P. (1971) *Duel of Eagles*, London: Simon & Schuster.

Tremblay, P. (1995) 'The Organizational Assets of the Learning Firm', *Human Systems Management*. 14: 7–20.

Tucker, J. (1755) *The Elements of Commerce, and Theory of Taxes*, London.

Turksen, I.B. (2000) 'Fuzzy Expert Systems', in M. Zeleny (ed.), *The IEBM Handbook of Information Technology in Business*, London: Thomson Learning: 330–339.

Urwick, L.F. (1933) *Management of Tomorrow*, London: Nisbet & Co.

Warner, M. (1984) *Organizations and Experiments*, Chichester: Wiley.

— (1987) 'Industrialization, Management Education and Training Systems: A Comparative Analysis', *Journal of Management Studies* 24 (1): 91–112.

— (ed.) (1999) *China's Managerial Revolution*, London: Frank Cass.

— (2001) 'Taylor, Frederick Winslow', in M. Warner (ed.), *International Encyclopedia of Business and Management*, London: Thomson Learning, 6364–6368.

Warner, M. and P. Joynt (eds) (2002), *Managing Across Cultures*, London: Thomson Learning.

Warner, M. and M. Witzel (1998) 'General Management Revisited', *Journal of General Management* 23 (4): 1–18.

— (1999) 'The Virtual General Manager', *Journal of General Management* 24 (4): 71–92.

— (2000) 'Finance and the Virtual Organisation', *Corporate Finance Review* (January–February): 1–10.

Weber, M. (1947) *The Protestant Ethic and the Spirit of Capitalism*, New York: Scribner's.

Weiss, H. and A. Wieandt (2000) 'Value-Based Management in Banking: A European Perspective', *Corporate Finance Review*, May–June: 14–27.

Williamson, O.E. (1985) *The Economic Institutions of Capitalism: Firms, Markets, Relational Contracting*, New York: The Free Press.

Witzel, M. (2000) 'Knowledge, Definitions of', in M. Zeleny (ed.), *The Handbook of Information Technology in Business*, London: Thomson Learning: 151–160.

— (2003) 'The Organic Organization: Harrington Emerson's Philosophy of Efficiency', paper presented to the Academy of International Business UK conference, De Montfort University, Leicester, 11 April 2003.

Wolff, M. (1999) *Burn Rate: How I Survived the Gold Rush Years on the Internet*, New York: Touchstone.

Zeleny, M. (2000) 'Introduction: What is IT/S?', in M. Zeleny (ed.), *The IEBM Handbook of Information Technology in Business*, London: Thomson Learning: xv–xvii.

Index